FOOD
FOR THE
SOUL

THE AUSTRALIAN Women's Weekly

FOOD FOR THE SOUL

THE AUSTRALIAN WOMEN'S WEEKLY
TRIPLE TESTED
TEST KITCHEN

CONTENTS

QUICK
COMFORT

QUICK
SOUPS

BROCCOLI & KALE SOUP WITH LEMON CRÈME FRAÎCHE

PREP + COOK TIME **30 MINUTES** SERVES **4**

200G (6½ OUNCES) KALE LEAVES, STEMS REMOVED, CHOPPED COARSELY

1½ TABLESPOONS OLIVE OIL

1 LARGE BROWN ONION (200G), CHOPPED FINELY

3 CLOVES GARLIC, CHOPPED FINELY

1.5 LITRES (6 CUPS) GOOD-QUALITY VEGETABLE STOCK

650G (1¼ POUNDS) SEBAGO POTATOES, CHOPPED

450G (14½ OUNCES) BROCCOLI, CUT INTO FLORETS, STEMS SLICED THINLY

1 CUP LOOSELY PACKED FRESH FLAT-LEAF PARSLEY LEAVES

1 CUP (240G) CRÈME FRAÎCHE

1 TABLESPOON FINELY GRATED LEMON RIND

SHREDDED LEMON RIND, TO SERVE

1 Preheat oven to 180°C/350°F.

2 Rub 50g (1½ ounces) of the kale with 2 teaspoons of the oil. Place on an oven tray. Bake for 10 minutes or until crisp.

3 Meanwhile, heat remaining oil in a large saucepan over medium heat; cook onion and garlic, stirring, for 5 minutes or until softened.

4 Add stock and potato; bring to the boil. Reduce heat to low; simmer, covered, for 5 minutes.

5 Add broccoli; simmer, covered, for 6 minutes or until vegetables are tender.

6 Stir in remaining kale and parsley; cook for a further 1 minute or until just wilted. Remove soup from heat. Using a stick blender, carefully blend the soup until smooth. Season to taste.

7 Combine crème fraîche and grated rind in a small bowl; season.

8 Ladle soup into bowls; top with crème fraîche mixture, kale chips and shredded rind.

tips Sebago is a white-fleshed potato. You can use any white all-purpose non-waxy potato for this recipe.

You can use chicken stock in place of vegetable stock, if you like.

If using a jug blender or food processor to blend soup, stand it for 10 minutes to cool slightly before blending. The heat build-up can cause the lid to blow off.

The soup, without crème fraîche, can be frozen for up to 3 months.

BEETROOT & GIN SOUP WITH PUMPERNICKEL CRUMBS

PREP + COOK TIME **50 MINUTES (+ STANDING)** SERVES **4**

50G (1½ OUNCES) BUTTER

¼ CUP (60ML) OLIVE OIL

1 LARGE BROWN ONION (200G), CHOPPED COARSELY

1KG (2 POUNDS) BEETROOT (BEETS), PEELED, GRATED COARSELY

1 LARGE POTATO (300G), CHOPPED COARSELY

1 MEDIUM FENNEL BULB (300G), CHOPPED COARSELY, FRONDS RESERVED

1 LARGE TOMATO (220G), CHOPPED COARSELY

1.75 LITRES (7 CUPS) VEGETABLE OR BEEF STOCK

3 SLICES PUMPERNICKEL BREAD (195G), TORN INTO COARSE CRUMBS

½ CUP (125ML) GIN

⅓ CUP (80G) SOUR CREAM

⅓ CUP (25G) FLAKED NATURAL ALMONDS, TOASTED

1 Heat butter and 1 tablespoon of the oil in a large saucepan over medium heat; cook onion, stirring occasionally, for 5 minutes or until soft. Add beetroot, potato, fennel and tomato; cook, stirring occasionally, for 10 minutes or until fennel is golden and caramelised. Stir in stock; bring to the boil. Reduce heat to low; simmer, covered, for 20 minutes or until potato and beetroot are tender. Remove from heat; stand for 10 minutes.

2 Blend or process soup, in batches, until smooth. Return soup to pan; stir over medium heat for 5 minutes or until hot.

3 Meanwhile, heat remaining oil in a medium frying pan over high heat; cook pumpernickel crumbs, stirring occasionally, for 2 minutes or until crumbs are crisp. Drain on paper towel.

4 Stir gin into hot soup; season.

5 Ladle soup into warm bowls; top with sour cream, pumpernickel crumbs, almonds and reserved fennel fronds.

tips This soup can also be served chilled.

Soup can be frozen after blending until smooth in step 2, for up to 3 months.

BULLSHOT WITH
PÂTÉ TOASTS

PREP + COOK TIME **25 MINUTES** SERVES **4**

2 TABLESPOONS OLIVE OIL
1 LARGE BROWN ONION (200G), SLICED THINLY
1.5 LITRES (6 CUPS) BEEF STOCK
⅓ CUP (80ML) VODKA
1 SMALL SEEDED BAGUETTE (175G), SLICED DIAGONALLY IN 1CM (½-INCH) SLICES
COOKING-OIL SPRAY
1 CLOVE GARLIC, PEELED, HALVED LENGTHWAYS
80G (2½ OUNCES) CHICKEN AND PEPPERCORN PÂTÉ

1 Heat oil in a medium saucepan over medium heat; cook onion, stirring occasionally, for 10 minutes or until softened and browned lightly. Stir in stock; bring to the boil. Stir in vodka; season to taste.

2 Meanwhile, coat both sides of bread slices with cooking-oil spray. Toast bread on a heated oiled grill plate (or grill or barbecue) over high heat for 1 minute each side or until golden brown. Rub hot toast with garlic; spread toast with pâté. Season with pepper.

3 Ladle soup into bowls, large mugs or heatproof jars; top with pâté toasts.

tips Use a good-quality store-bought or homemade beef stock for this recipe.

Use your favourite pâté, if you like.

Soup can be frozen for up to 3 months.

CHEAT'S PEA & HAM SOUP

PREP + COOK TIME **35 MINUTES** SERVES **4**

40G (1½ OUNCES) BUTTER, CHOPPED

3 GREEN ONIONS (SCALLIONS), SLICED THINLY

1 CLOVE GARLIC, CHOPPED FINELY

1 LARGE POTATO (200G), CHOPPED

1.5 LITRES (6 CUPS) CHICKEN STOCK

1 CUP (250ML) WATER

6 CUPS (720G) FROZEN PEAS

⅔ CUP LOOSELY PACKED FRESH MINT LEAVES

1 TABLESPOON OLIVE OIL

300G (9½ OUNCES) SLICED LEG HAM

½ CUP (125ML) POURING CREAM

SNOW PEA SPROUTS, TO SERVE

1 Heat butter in a large saucepan over medium-low heat; cook green onion and garlic, stirring, for 5 minutes or until softened.

2 Add potato, stock and the water; bring to the boil. Reduce heat to medium-low; simmer, covered, for 10 minutes or until tender. Add 5 cups (600g) of the peas; cook for a further 2 minutes or until peas are just tender. Remove pan from heat.

3 Add mint; blend with a stick blender until smooth. Add remaining peas; stir over medium-low heat until hot. Season to taste. Reduce heat to low; cover, to keep warm.

4 Heat oil in a large frying pan over medium heat; cook ham for 2 minutes each side or until golden brown and crisp.

5 Ladle soup into bowls; drizzle with cream. Top with torn ham and pea sprouts.

tips *If using a blender or food processor to blend soup, stand it for 10 minutes to cool slightly before blending. The heat build-up can cause the lid to blow off.*

This soup can be frozen for up to 3 months.

CREAMY CELERIAC SOUP WITH SCALLOPS

PREP + COOK TIME **50 MINUTES** SERVES **4**

50G (1½ OUNCES) BUTTER

2 TABLESPOONS EXTRA VIRGIN OLIVE OIL

1 MEDIUM BROWN ONION (150G), CHOPPED COARSELY

1KG (2 POUNDS) CELERIAC (CELERY ROOT), PEELED, CHOPPED COARSELY

1 STALK CELERY (150G), TRIMMED, CHOPPED

2 CLOVES GARLIC, QUARTERED

1.25 LITRES (5 CUPS) SALT-REDUCED VEGETABLE STOCK

8 SCALLOPS WITHOUT ROE (200G)

4 RINDLESS BACON SLICES (250G), HALVED LENGTHWAYS

¼ CUP (60ML) POURING CREAM

1 TABLESPOON LEMON JUICE

1 TABLESPOON FRESH THYME LEAVES

1 Heat half the butter and half the oil in a large saucepan over medium heat; cook onion, celeriac, celery and garlic, stirring occasionally, for 10 minutes or until softened. Stir in stock; bring to the boil. Reduce heat to low; simmer, covered, for 20 minutes or until celeriac is tender. Cool for 10 minutes.

2 Meanwhile, wrap each scallop with a strip of bacon; secure with toothpicks. Cover; refrigerate until required.

3 Blend or process soup, in batches, until smooth. Return soup to pan with cream; stir over medium heat until hot. Season to taste. Cover to keep warm.

4 Melt remaining butter and oil in a large frying pan over high heat. Season scallops; cook scallops for 2 minutes on first side and 1 minute on second side or until scallops are almost cooked through. Transfer to a plate. Remove pan from heat; stir in juice.

5 Ladle soup into warm bowls. Remove toothpicks, top with scallops and thyme. Drizzle with lemon mixture.

tips You can use scallops with the roe, if you like.

The soup can be frozen at the end of step 1.

VEGETABLE
LAKSA
(See recipe page 22)

photograph page 21

VEGETABLE LAKSA

PREP + COOK TIME **25 MINUTES** SERVES **4**

½ CUP (150G) LAKSA PASTE

1 LITRE (4 CUPS) VEGETABLE
   STOCK

1⅔ CUPS (400ML) CANNED
   COCONUT MILK

1 LEMON GRASS STALK,
   GRATED FINELY

2 FRESH KAFFIR LIME LEAVES,
   SHREDDED FINELY

1 LARGE CARROT (180G),
   SLICED INTO RIBBONS

100G (3 OUNCES) SNOW PEAS,
   HALVED DIAGONALLY

1 BABY BUK CHOY (250G),
   LEAVES TORN,
   STEMS CHOPPED

200G (6½ OUNCES) FRIED
   TOFU PUFFS

1 TABLESPOON FISH SAUCE

2 TEASPOONS BROWN SUGAR

1 TABLESPOON LIME JUICE

100G (3 OUNCES) DRIED THICK
   RICE STICK NOODLES

⅓ CUP (25G) BEAN SPROUTS

½ CUP LOOSELY PACKED
   THAI BASIL LEAVES

1 LONG FRESH RED CHILLI,
   SLICED THINLY

1 LIME (90G),
   CUT INTO WEDGES

1 Heat a wok over a high heat. Add laksa paste; cook, stirring, for 1 minute or until fragrant. Add stock, coconut milk, lemon grass and lime leaves; bring to the boil, add carrot. Reduce heat; simmer, uncovered, for 3 minutes or until carrot is just tender. Add snow peas, buk choy and tofu; simmer, uncovered, for 1 minute. Stir in fish sauce, sugar and juice. Season to taste.

2 Meanwhile, place noodles in a heatproof bowl, add enough boiling water to cover; stand for 5 minutes or until tender. Stir to separate strands. Drain. Divide noodles between serving bowls.

3 Ladle laksa over noodles. Serve topped with bean sprouts, basil and chilli; accompany with lime wedges.

tips For a vegetarian laksa, check the label of the paste to make sure it doesn't contain fish sauce or shrimp paste. Also, use soy sauce instead of fish sauce.

If you can't find fried tofu puffs, use silken tofu instead and heat through gently.

Recipe is not suitable to freeze.

photograph page 24

THAI RED CURRY KUMARA SOUP

PREP + COOK TIME **35 MINUTES (+ STANDING)** SERVES **4**

1 TABLESPOON VEGETABLE OIL

1 LARGE BROWN ONION (200G), CHOPPED

2 TABLESPOONS RED CURRY PASTE

1 TABLESPOON GRATED FRESH GINGER

2 TEASPOONS FINELY CHOPPED TRIMMED CORIANDER (CILANTRO) ROOTS

1KG (2 POUNDS) KUMARA (ORANGE SWEET POTATO), PEELED, CUT INTO CHUNKS

1 LITRE (4 CUPS) VEGETABLE STOCK

1 CUP (250ML) WATER

1 TABLESPOON FISH SAUCE

1 TABLESPOON LIME JUICE

2 TEASPOONS BROWN SUGAR

¾ CUP (200G) COCONUT YOGHURT

½ CUP BABY SHISO LEAVES

1 TABLESPOON FRIED SHALLOTS

LIME CHEEKS, TO SERVE

1 Heat oil in a large saucepan over medium-high heat; cook onion, stirring, for 5 minutes or until softened. Add curry paste, ginger and coriander roots; cook, stirring, for 1 minute or until fragrant.

2 Add kumara, stock and the water; bring to the boil. Reduce heat to low; simmer, covered, for 15 minutes or until kumara is tender. Remove from heat; stand 5 minutes. Blend soup until smooth using a stick blender.

3 Add fish sauce, juice, sugar and yoghurt; stir over medium heat until hot. Season to taste.

4 Ladle soup into bowls; top with shiso leaves and shallots. Serve with lime cheeks.

tips *You can use a jug blender for a smoother consistency.*

Recipe is suitable to freeze at the end of step 2.

THAI RED CURRY
KUMARA SOUP
(See recipe page 23)

HEARTY CURRIED
VEGETABLE &
CHICKPEA SOUP

PREP + COOK TIME **50 MINUTES** SERVES **4**

- 1 TABLESPOON OLIVE OIL
- 2 CLOVES GARLIC, CRUSHED
- 2 TEASPOONS FINELY GRATED FRESH GINGER
- 1 LARGE BROWN ONION (200G), CHOPPED
- 300G (9½ OUNCES) PUMPKIN, CUT INTO 2CM (¾-INCH) CUBES
- 1 MEDIUM POTATO (200G), CUT INTO 2CM (¾-INCH) CUBES
- 2 MEDIUM CARROTS (240G), CHOPPED COARSELY
- 1 TABLESPOON CURRY POWDER
- 2 TEASPOONS CUMIN SEEDS, TOASTED (SEE TIPS)
- 1 LITRE (4 CUPS) VEGETABLE STOCK
- 200G (6½ OUNCES) CAULIFLOWER, CUT INTO SMALL FLORETS
- 440G (14 OUNCES) CANNED CHICKPEAS (GARBANZO BEANS), DRAINED, RINSED
- 4 PAPPADAMS
- ⅓ CUP (95G) GREEK-STYLE YOGHURT
- 1 TABLESPOON BABY CORIANDER LEAVES

1 Heat oil in a large saucepan over medium heat; cook garlic, ginger, onion, pumpkin, potato and carrot, stirring, for 5 minutes or until vegetables have softened. Add curry powder and half the cumin seeds; cook, stirring, until fragrant.

2 Stir in stock and bring to the boil; reduce heat, simmer, uncovered, for 20 minutes or until vegetables are just tender. Stir in cauliflower and chickpeas; simmer, uncovered, for 15 minutes until cauliflower is tender. Season to taste.

3 Microwave pappadams on HIGH (100%) for 30 seconds or until puffed.

4 Ladle soup into bowls; top with yoghurt, coriander and remaining cumin seeds. Serve soup with pappadams.

tips To toast cumin seeds, stir seeds in a small frying pan over medium heat for 2 minutes or until fragrant; remove from heat.

The pumpkin will break down and thicken the soup.

The soup is suitable to freeze at the end of step 2.

ROASTED TOMATO SOUP WITH BROCCOLI PESTO

PREP + COOK TIME **1 HOUR (+ STANDING)** SERVES **4**

1KG (2 POUNDS) VINE-RIPENED TOMATOES, QUARTERED

3 CLOVES GARLIC, UNPEELED

3 SPRIGS FRESH THYME

1 MEDIUM BROWN ONION (150G), CHOPPED

½ TEASPOON SEA SALT FLAKES

¼ CUP (60ML) EXTRA VIRGIN OLIVE OIL

3 CUPS (750ML) CHICKEN STOCK

1 TABLESPOON PINE NUTS, TOASTED

BABY BASIL LEAVES, TO SERVE

BROCCOLI PESTO

100G (3 OUNCES) BROCCOLI, CHOPPED

1 CLOVE GARLIC, CRUSHED

1½ TABLESPOONS PINE NUTS, TOASTED

1½ TABLESPOONS GRATED PARMESAN

1½ TABLESPOONS COARSELY CHOPPED FRESH BASIL LEAVES

¼ CUP (60ML) OLIVE OIL

1 Preheat oven to 220°C/425°F.
2 Place tomatoes, garlic, thyme and onion in a baking dish; sprinkle with salt flakes, season with freshly ground black pepper. Drizzle with oil; toss to coat tomatoes. Roast for 30 minutes or until tomatoes are very soft and coloured around the edges.
3 Meanwhile, make broccoli pesto.
4 Transfer roasted tomato mixture to a medium saucepan. Squeeze garlic out of skins and add garlic to tomato mixture. Remove thyme stalks. Add stock to pan and bring to the boil; remove from heat. Stand 10 minutes to cool slightly. Blend or process mixture until smooth. Return soup to pan; stir over low heat until hot. Season.
5 Ladle soup into bowls; top with broccoli pesto, pine nuts, basil and extra fresh tomato, if you like,

broccoli pesto Add broccoli to a small saucepan of boiling water. Bring to the boil; simmer, uncovered, for 2 minutes. Drain; refresh in cold water, drain well. Process broccoli, garlic, pine nuts, parmesan and basil until finely chopped. With motor operating, gradually pour in oil; process until combined. Season to taste.

tips Use vegetable stock instead of chicken stock, if you prefer.

Soup and broccoli pesto are suitable to freeze, separately, for up to 3 months.

CREAMY CORN
& CRAB SOUP

PREP + COOK TIME **40 MINUTES (+ STANDING)** SERVES **4**

20G (¾ OUNCE) BUTTER

2 MEDIUM BROWN ONIONS (300G), CHOPPED COARSELY

3 CUPS (500G) FROZEN CORN KERNELS, THAWED

1 TABLESPOON CHOPPED FRESH CORIANDER (CILANTRO) ROOTS

1 LITRE (4 CUPS) VEGETABLE STOCK

300ML POURING CREAM

½ CUP (120G) SOUR CREAM

140G (4½ OUNCES) COOKED CRAB MEAT

2 TABLESPOONS FRESH CORIANDER (CILANTRO) LEAVES

1 TABLESPOON SWEET SHERRY

1 Melt butter in a large saucepan over medium heat; cook onion, corn and coriander roots, stirring, for 10 minutes or until onion is soft.

2 Add stock; simmer, uncovered, for 15 minutes or until vegetables are tender. Stand for 10 minutes to cool slightly.

3 Blend or process soup until smooth. Return soup to pan with cream. Stir over low heat until hot; season to taste.

4 Ladle soup into bowls; top with sour cream, crab and coriander. Drizzle with sherry. Season with ground black pepper.

tips *You will need to buy 1 bunch coriander for the coriander roots.*

The soup is suitable to freeze at the end of step 2.

QUICK
PASTA & RICE

BROWN RICE & MUSHROOM BOWL WITH DUKKAH EGGS

PREP + COOK TIME **45 MINUTES** SERVES **4**

1⅓ CUPS (265G) BROWN RICE

4 EGGS (SEE TIPS)

¼ CUP (60ML) EXTRA VIRGIN OLIVE OIL

1 SMALL BROWN ONION (80G), CHOPPED FINELY

2 CLOVES GARLIC, CRUSHED

200G (6½ OUNCES) SWISS BROWN MUSHROOMS

4 KALE LEAVES (100G), STEMS REMOVED, TORN COARSELY

1 TABLESPOON BLACK SESAME SEEDS

2 TABLESPOONS DUKKAH

1 Cook rice in a medium saucepan of boiling salted water, uncovered, for 25 minutes or until just tender; drain.

2 Meanwhile, add refrigerated eggs to a saucepan of boiling water; boil, uncovered, for 5 minutes for soft-boiled. Drain; rinse eggs under cold water until cool enough to handle. Peel eggs.

3 Heat oil in a large non-stick frying pan over medium heat. Cook onion, stirring, for 5 minutes or until softened. Add garlic and mushrooms; cook, stirring occasionally, for a further 5 minutes or until mushrooms are browned. Add kale; cook, stirring, for 3 minutes or until kale is wilted. Stir in rice; season to taste.

4 Combine seeds and dukkah in a small bowl; roll eggs in the mixture to coat. Divide rice mixture between serving bowls. Top with eggs and remaining dukkah mixture.

tips There's no need to bring the eggs to room temperature. Add them to the boiling water straight from the fridge.

You could use a mixture of mushrooms such as swiss brown, portobello, button or shiitake mushrooms.

Recipe is not suitable to freeze.

TUNA, SPINACH & BROCCOLINI BAKED RISOTTO

PREP + COOK TIME **50 MINUTES** SERVES **4**

1 TABLESPOON EXTRA VIRGIN OLIVE OIL
100G (3 OUNCES) BACON SLICES, RIND REMOVED, CHOPPED COARSELY
1 CLOVE GARLIC, CRUSHED
1½ CUPS (300G) ARBORIO RICE
3½ CUPS (875ML) CHICKEN STOCK
175G (5½ OUNCES) BROCCOLINI, TRIMMED, THICK STEMS HALVED LENGTHWAYS
50G (1½ OUNCES) BABY SPINACH LEAVES
40G (1½ OUNCES) BUTTER, CHOPPED
425G (13½ OUNCES) CANNED TUNA IN OIL, DRAINED
1 CUP (80G) FINELY GRATED PARMESAN
SHREDDED LEMON RIND, TO SERVE

1 Preheat oven to 180°C/350°F.
2 Heat oil in a large heavy-based flameproof ovenproof saucepan or dish over medium heat; cook bacon, stirring, for 2 minutes or until browned. Add garlic; cook, stirring, until fragrant. Stir in rice and stock.
3 Cover pan with lid; transfer to oven, bake for 35 minutes. Remove pan from oven, add broccolini, cover; return to oven for 4 minutes or until broccolini is tender.
4 Stir in spinach, butter, tuna and half the parmesan. Season.
5 Combine rind and remaining parmesan; sprinkle over risotto just before serving.

tips Broccolini can be substituted with asparagus in this recipe.

Leftover cold risotto can be rolled into balls, rolled in dry breadcrumbs and deep-fried until golden. Serve balls as a starter or with salad for a light lunch.

Recipe is not suitable to freeze.

MEXICAN
RICE BOWL
(See recipe page 40)

photograph page 39

MEXICAN RICE BOWL

PREP + COOK TIME **35 MINUTES** SERVES **4**

2 TABLESPOONS OLIVE OIL

1 SMALL RED ONION (100G), SLICED

2 CLOVES GARLIC, CRUSHED

500G (1 POUND) CHICKEN THIGH FILLETS, CHOPPED

1 CURED CHORIZO SAUSAGE (100G), SLICED

1 MEDIUM RED CAPSICUM (BELL PEPPER) (200G), SLICED THICKLY

2 TABLESPOONS TOMATO PASTE

1 TEASPOON DRIED OREGANO LEAVES

1 TEASPOON GROUND CUMIN

1 TEASPOON SMOKED PAPRIKA

1 TEASPOON GROUND CORIANDER

2 CUPS (500ML) CHICKEN STOCK

400G (12½ OUNCES) CANNED CRUSHED TOMATOES

1½ CUPS (300G) LONG GRAIN WHITE RICE

400G (12½ OUNCES) CANNED RED KIDNEY BEANS, DRAINED, RINSED

1 CORN COB (400G), HUSK AND SILK REMOVED

1 LONG FRESH RED CHILLI, SLICED

½ CUP LOOSELY PACKED FRESH CORIANDER (CILANTRO) LEAVES

1 MEDIUM AVOCADO (250G), SLICED

1 Heat oil in a large deep frying pan over high heat. Cook onion and garlic, stirring, for 3 minutes or until soft. Add the chicken; cook, stirring for 5 minutes or until browned.

2 Add chorizo and capsicum; cook, stirring, for 3 minutes or until browned. Stir in paste, oregano and spices; cook, stirring, for 2 minutes. Add stock, tomatoes and rice; bring to the boil. Reduce heat to low; simmer, covered, for 15 minutes or until liquid is absorbed. Stir in beans; season to taste.

3 Meanwhile, cook corn on a heated oiled grill plate (or grill or barbecue) over medium heat, turning occasionally, for 8 minutes or until charred. Cool slightly, then remove kernels from cob using a small sharp knife.

4 Divide mixture between serving bowls. Top with corn, chilli, coriander leaves and avocado. Serve with toasted tortillas and lime cheeks, if you like

tip Recipe is not suitable to freeze.

photograph page 42

BEETROOT, HALOUMI & RICE
WINTER SALAD

PREP + COOK TIME **25 MINUTES** SERVES **4**

- 1 CUP (200G) BROWN RICE
- ⅓ CUP (80ML) EXTRA VIRGIN OLIVE OIL
- 1 SMALL RED ONION (100G), CUT INTO WEDGES
- 1 TEASPOON GROUND CUMIN
- 1 TEASPOON GROUND CORIANDER
- 400G (12½ OUNCES) CANNED CHICKPEAS (GARBANZO BEANS), DRAINED, RINSED
- 500G (1 POUND) PACKAGED PRE-COOKED BEETROOT (BEETS), QUARTERED
- 100G (3 OUNCES) BABY SPINACH LEAVES
- 1 CUP LOOSELY PACKED FRESH MINT LEAVES, TORN
- ½ CUP (50G) WALNUTS, TOASTED, CHOPPED COARSELY
- 2 TABLESPOONS BALSAMIC GLAZE
- 200G (6½ OUNCES) HALOUMI, SLICED

1 Cook rice in a large saucepan of boiling salted water, uncovered, for 20 minutes or until just tender; drain.

2 Meanwhile, heat 1 tablespoon of the oil in a large frying pan over medium heat. Add onion; cook, stirring, for 5 minutes or until tender. Add cumin and coriander; cook, stirring, for 30 seconds or until fragrant. Add chickpeas and beetroot; stir until heated through.

3 Meanwhile, combine rice, spinach, mint and nuts in a large bowl. Drizzle with combined 1 tablespoon of the balsamic glaze and 2 tablespoons of the remaining oil. Add beetroot and chickpea mixture; season to taste and mix gently.

4 Heat remaining oil in a large frying pan over high heat. Cook haloumi for 2 minutes each side or until golden.

5 Serve salad with haloumi, drizzled with remaining balsamic glaze.

tips You can replace the haloumi with uncooked crumbled goat's cheese or fetta.

Recipe is not suitable to freeze.

BEETROOT, HALOUMI
& RICE WINTER SALAD
(See recipe page 41)

BAKED CHILLI BOCCONCINI & SQUID INK SPAGHETTI

PREP + COOK TIME **25 MINUTES** SERVES **4**

- 500G (1 POUND) SQUID INK SPAGHETTI
- 200G (6½ OUNCES) BOCCONCINI, DRAINED
- ¼ CUP (60ML) EXTRA VIRGIN OLIVE OIL
- 1 LONG FRESH RED CHILLI, CHOPPED FINELY
- 2 CLOVES GARLIC, CRUSHED
- 1 TEASPOON FINELY GRATED LEMON RIND
- ⅓ CUP (55G) DRY-ROASTED ALMOND KERNELS, CHOPPED COARSELY
- 2 TABLESPOONS FRESH FLAT-LEAF PARSLEY LEAVES

1 Preheat oven to 240°C/475°F. Grease a 2-litre (8-cup) ovenproof dish.

2 Cook spaghetti in a large saucepan of boiling salted water until tender; drain.

3 Meanwhile, combine bocconcini, oil, chilli, garlic, rind and almonds in a large bowl. Season to taste.

4 Add spaghetti to bocconcini mixture; toss gently to combine. Place in ovenproof dish. Bake for 5 minutes or until bocconcini is just starting to melt.

5 Serve immediately, sprinkled with parsley. Accompany with lemon cheeks, if you like.

tips You can use plain spaghetti, if you prefer.

Once the bocconcini is out of the oven, it is important to work quickly as it begins to set as it cools.

Recipe is not suitable to freeze.

CHORIZO &
POACHED EGG
TAGLIATELLE

PREP + COOK TIME **30 MINUTES** SERVES **4**

3 FRESH CHORIZO SAUSAGES (450G)
⅓ CUP (80ML) EXTRA VIRGIN OLIVE OIL
2 CLOVES GARLIC, CRUSHED
500G (1 POUND) TAGLIATELLE PASTA
2 TABLESPOONS WHITE VINEGAR
4 EGGS
¾ CUP (60G) COARSELY GRATED PARMESAN
2 TABLESPOONS FINELY CHOPPED FRESH FLAT-LEAF PARSLEY

1 Remove chorizo from their casings; finely chop sausage meat until it resembles mince.

2 Heat 1 tablespoon of the oil in a large frying pan over high heat; cook chorizo, stirring occasionally, for 4 minutes or until golden. Add garlic; cook, stirring, for 1 minute. Remove pan from heat; cover to keep warm.

3 Meanwhile, cook pasta in a large saucepan of boiling salted water until tender. Drain, reserving ¼ cup (60ml) cooking liquid. Return pasta to pan; cover to keep warm.

4 Half-fill a large frying pan with water; bring to the boil. Stir in vinegar. Break one egg into a cup, then slide into pan; repeat with remaining eggs. When all eggs are in pan, return water to the boil. Cover pan, turn off heat; stand for 4 minutes or until a light film of egg white sets over yolks.

Remove eggs, one at a time, using a slotted spoon; place spoon on paper towel-lined plate briefly to blot up any poaching liquid.

5 Working quickly, add chorizo mixture to pasta with half the parmesan, remaining oil and enough reserved cooking liquid to create a coating consistency; season to taste.

6 Serve pasta topped with eggs, remaining parmesan and parsley.

tips *Try to get the freshest free-range eggs available when poaching as the whites will set better and keep their shape.*

Recipe is not suitable to freeze.

PUMPKIN, SAGE & CAMEMBERT BAKED RISOTTO

PREP + COOK TIME **1 HOUR** SERVES **4**

- **3½ CUPS (875ML) PREPARED PUMPKIN SOUP**
- **2 CUPS (500ML) SALT-REDUCED VEGETABLE STOCK**
- **2 TABLESPOONS OLIVE OIL**
- **1 LARGE BROWN ONION (300G), CHOPPED FINELY**
- **2 CLOVES GARLIC, CRUSHED**
- **5 FRESH SAGE LEAVES**
- **1½ CUPS (300G) ARBORIO RICE**
- **¾ CUP (60G) SHAVED PARMESAN**
- **350G (11 OUNCES) JAP PUMPKIN, SLICED THINLY INTO WEDGES**
- **250G (8-OUNCE) WHOLE CAMEMBERT CHEESE**
- **2 TABLESPOONS OLIVE OIL, EXTRA**
- **12 FRESH SAGE LEAVES, EXTRA**
- **60G (2 OUNCES) TRIMMED WATERCRESS**
- **1 TABLESPOON LEMON JUICE**
- **⅓ CUP (45G) ROASTED HAZELNUTS, CHOPPED COARSELY**

1 Preheat oven to 180°C/350°F.

2 Bring soup and stock to the boil in a medium saucepan. Reduce heat; simmer, covered.

3 Meanwhile, heat oil in a medium frying pan over medium heat; cook onion, garlic and sage, stirring occasionally, for 5 minutes or until onion softens. Add rice; stir to coat in onion mixture. Stir in soup mixture and half the parmesan; season to taste.

4 Spoon risotto mixture into a 2.5-litre (10-cup) shallow ovenproof dish. Top with pumpkin wedges, pushing wedges in slightly; place camembert in the centre. Cover dish with foil.

5 Bake risotto for 15 minutes, stirring gently halfway through cooking time without disturbing the camembert. Bake for a further 25 minutes or until rice and pumpkin are tender.

6 Meanwhile, heat extra oil in a small frying pan over medium heat; cook extra sage leaves for 1 minute or until crisp. Drain on paper towel.

7 Combine watercress and juice in a medium bowl; season to taste.

8 Serve risotto topped with hazelnuts, crisp sage leaves and remaining parmesan; accompany with the watercress mixture.

tips *You can use brie instead of camembert, if you like.*

Recipe is not suitable to freeze.

MUSHROOM ORECCHIETTE WITH GREMOLATA CRUMBS

PREP + COOK TIME **50 MINUTES** SERVES **4**

30G (1 OUNCE) BUTTER
1 TABLESPOON OLIVE OIL
1 MEDIUM BROWN ONION
   (150G), CHOPPED FINELY
2 CLOVES GARLIC, CRUSHED
½ CUP (125ML) WHITE WINE
200G (6½ OUNCES) SWISS
   BROWN MUSHROOMS,
   SLICED
300ML POURING CREAM
200G (6½ OUNCES) SLICED
   PANCETTA
500G (1 POUND) DRY
   ORECCHIETTE PASTA

GREMOLATA CRUMBS
30G (1 OUNCE) BUTTER
1 CIABATTA ROLL (100G),
   TORN COARSELY
2 CLOVES GARLIC, CRUSHED
2 TABLESPOONS CHOPPED
   FRESH FLAT-LEAF PARSLEY
2 TEASPOONS FINELY GRATED
   LEMON RIND

1 Heat butter and oil in a medium frying pan; cook onion and garlic, stirring, for 5 minutes or until onion is soft. Add wine to pan; boil, uncovered, until reduced by half. Stir in mushrooms; cook, stirring occasionally, over medium heat, for 5 minutes or until softened. Add cream, stir over medium heat for 2 minutes or until thickened slightly. Season to taste; cover to keep warm.

2 Meanwhile, preheat oven to 180°C/350°F. Place pancetta, in a single layer on an oven tray lined with baking paper. Bake for 10 minutes or until golden and crisp.

3 Make gremolata crumbs.

4 Cook pasta in a large saucepan of boiling salted water until just tender. Drain, reserving ¼ cup (60ml) of cooking water. Return pasta to pan.

5 Add hot sauce to pasta; toss gently to combine. If mixture is a little thick, add some of the reserved pasta water. Serve pasta topped with crumbled pancetta, and gremolata crumbs.

gremolata crumbs Heat butter in a small saucepan over medium heat; add torn bread and garlic. Cook, stirring, for 2 minutes or until bread is golden brown. Remove from heat; stir in parsley and rind.

tips *You can use button mushrooms for a mild flavour, if you prefer.*

Recipe is not suitable to freeze.

serving suggestion *Serve with a green salad.*

CRUNCHY
MAC & CHEESE

PREP + COOK TIME **50 MINUTES** SERVES **4**

60G (2 OUNCES) BUTTER

¼ CUP (35G) PLAIN
(ALL-PURPOSE) FLOUR

1.25 LITRES (5 CUPS) MILK

PINCH FRESHLY GRATED
NUTMEG

1 CUP (80G) GRATED
PARMESAN

⅓ CUP (40G) GRATED
GRUYÈRE

⅓ CUP (40G) GRATED
CHEDDAR

400G (12½ OUNCES)
MACARONI PASTA

200G (6½ OUNCES)
SPECK, CUT INTO
1CM (½-INCH) PIECES

20G (¾ OUNCE) BUTTER,
EXTRA

150G (4½ OUNCES)
SOURDOUGH BREAD,
CRUST REMOVED, TORN
INTO SMALL CHUNKS

1 TABLESPOON
COARSLEY CHOPPED
FRESH FLAT-LEAF PARSLEY

1 Preheat oven to 180°C/350°F. Lightly grease a 2.5-litre (10-cup) ovenproof dish.

2 Melt butter in a large saucepan over medium heat. Add flour; cook, stirring until mixture bubbles. Gradually stir in milk, stirring constantly until all the milk is incorporated and sauce is smooth. Add nutmeg; cook, stirring until mixture boils and thickens. Remove pan from heat; add cheeses, mix well. Season to taste.

3 Meanwhile, cook pasta in a large saucepan of boiling salted boiling water for 5 minutes or until just tender. Drain.

4 Heat a large frying pan over medium heat; cook speck and extra butter, stirring, for 5 minutes or until lightly browned. Add half the speck to the cheese sauce. Add sourdough to remaining speck; stir until well combined.

5 Stir pasta into cheese sauce. Pour mixture into ovenproof dish. Sprinkle with bread mixture. Bake for 20 minutes or until bread is golden and crisp. Sprinkle with parsley.

tips *You could also make this recipe in 2 x 1.25-litre (5-cup) ovenproof dishes, if you prefer.*

Make child-friendly by omitting the gruyère and increasing the cheddar.

Recipe is not suitable to freeze.

RICOTTA GNOCCHI WITH SALAMI

PREP + COOK TIME **45 MINUTES** SERVES **4**

- 500G (1 POUND) BABY ROMA (EGG) TOMATOES
- 2 TABLESPOONS EXTRA VIRGIN OLIVE OIL
- 2 CLOVES GARLIC, CRUSHED
- 2 TEASPOONS DRIED OREGANO LEAVES
- 2 TEASPOONS WHITE BALSAMIC VINEGAR
- ½ TEASPOON DRIED CHILLI FLAKES
- 500G (1 POUND) FULL-CREAM RICOTTA
- 1½ CUPS (120G) FINELY GRATED PARMESAN
- 1 EGG, BEATEN LIGHTLY
- 2 TABLESPOONS CHOPPED FRESH BASIL
- 1 CUP (150G) PLAIN (ALL-PURPOSE) FLOUR, APPROXIMATELY
- 100G (3 OUNCES) THINLY SLICED HOT SALAMI, HALVED
- 250G (8 OUNCES) MASCARPONE
- ¼ CUP (20G) SHAVED PARMESAN, EXTRA
- ¼ CUP LOOSELY PACKED FRESH BASIL LEAVES, EXTRA

1 Preheat oven to 180°C/350°F. Line a 25cm x 35cm (10-inch x 14-inch) oven tray with baking paper.

2 Combine tomatoes, oil, garlic, oregano, balsamic and chilli in a medium bowl; season. Spread mixture onto prepared tray. Bake for 15 minutes or until lightly browned.

3 Meanwhile, place ricotta in a medium bowl. Stir in grated parmesan, egg and chopped basil; season well. Add enough of the flour to mix to a soft dough; do not over-mix. Divide dough in half. Roll each half on a lightly floured work surface into a 2cm (¾-inch) thick rope. Using a floured butter knife, cut dough into 2cm (¾-inch) lengths.

4 Cook gnocchi in two batches in a large saucepan of boiling salted water. Once gnocchi rise to the surface, cook for a further 1 minute. Using a slotted spoon, transfer gnocchi to oven tray with tomatoes; stir to distribute gnocchi through tomato mixture.

5 Preheat grill (broiler) on high.

6 Top gnocchi with salami and dollops of mascarpone. Grill for 10 minutes or until browned lightly.

7 Serve sprinkled with extra parmesan and basil.

tips You can omit the chilli and use a mild salami or ham, if you prefer.

Recipe is not suitable to freeze.

PRESSURE COOKER

BUTTER CHICKEN

PREP + COOK TIME **40 MINUTES** SERVES **4**

4 CHICKEN MARYLANDS (1.4KG)
1 TABLESPOON LEMON JUICE
½ CUP (140G) YOGHURT
5CM (2-INCH) PIECE FRESH GINGER (25G), GRATED
2 TEASPOONS GARAM MASALA
1 TABLESPOON VEGETABLE OIL
40G (1½ OUNCES) BUTTER
1 MEDIUM BROWN ONION (150G), CHOPPED FINELY
4 CLOVES GARLIC, CRUSHED
1 TEASPOON EACH GROUND CORIANDER, CUMIN, CINNAMON AND HOT PAPRIKA
2 TABLESPOONS TOMATO PASTE
410G (13 OUNCES) CANNED TOMATO PUREE
½ CUP (125ML) CHICKEN STOCK
2 TABLESPOONS HONEY
⅓ CUP (80ML) POURING CREAM
½ CUP LOOSELY PACKED FRESH CORIANDER (CILANTRO) LEAVES

1 Combine chicken, juice, yoghurt, ginger and garam masala in a large bowl. Heat half the oil and half the butter in a 6-litre (24-cup) pressure cooker; cook chicken, in batches, until browned. Remove from cooker.
2 Heat remaining oil and butter in cooker; cook onion and garlic, stirring, for 5 minutes or until onion softens. Add spices; cook, stirring, for 1 minute or until fragrant. Return chicken to cooker with paste, puree, stock and honey; secure lid. Bring cooker to high pressure. Reduce heat to stabilise pressure; cook for 20 minutes.
3 Release pressure using the quick release method (see tips); remove lid. Stir in cream; season to taste. Serve chicken sprinkled with coriander.

tips If you have an electric pressure cooker you won't need to reduce the heat to stabilise pressure, your cooker will automatically stabilise itself. Always check with the manufacturer's instructions before using. For the quick release method referred to, use tongs (steam can burn your fingers) to turn the pressure valve on top of the cooker to open the valve and release the steam (this releases the pressure quickly before you remove the lid).

Recipe is not suitable to freeze.

serving suggestion Serve with steamed basmati rice.

BEEF TAGINE
WITH SPINACH
& OLIVES

PREP + COOK TIME **30 MINUTES** SERVES **4**

1 TABLESPOON OLIVE OIL

1.2KG (2½ POUNDS) BEEF BLADE STEAK, TRIMMED, CHOPPED COARSELY

1 MEDIUM BROWN ONION (150G), CHOPPED FINELY

2 CLOVES GARLIC, CRUSHED

1 TEASPOON GROUND ALLSPICE

1 TEASPOON DRIED CHILLI FLAKES

PINCH SAFFRON THREADS

410G (13 OUNCES) CANNED CRUSHED TOMATOES

½ CUP (125ML) BEEF STOCK

300G (9½ OUNCES) SPINACH, TRIMMED, SHREDDED COARSELY

½ CUP (60G) SEEDED GREEN OLIVES

2 TABLESPOONS THINLY SLICED PRESERVED LEMON RIND

⅓ CUP (45G) COARSELY CHOPPED, ROASTED UNSALTED PISTACHIOS

1 Heat half the oil in a 6-litre (24-cup) pressure cooker; cook beef, in batches, until browned. Remove from cooker.

2 Heat remaining oil in cooker; cook onion, garlic and spices, stirring, for 3 minutes or until onion softens. Return beef to cooker with tomatoes and stock; secure lid. Bring cooker to high pressure. Reduce heat to stabilise pressure; cook for 15 minutes.

3 Release pressure using the quick release method (see tips); remove lid. Stir in spinach, olives and preserved lemon; simmer, uncovered, until hot. Season.

4 Serve tagine sprinkled with pistachios.

tips *If you have an electric pressure cooker you won't need to reduce the heat to stabilise pressure, your cooker will automatically stabilise itself. Always check with the manufacturer's instructions before using. For the quick release method referred to, use tongs (steam can burn your fingers) to turn the pressure valve on top of the cooker to open the valve and release the steam (this releases the pressure quickly before you remove the lid).*

Recipe is not suitable to freeze.

serving suggestion
Serve with couscous.

BOEUF BOURGUIGNON

PREP + COOK TIME **1 HOUR** SERVES **6**

1½ TABLESPOONS OLIVE OIL

400G (12½ OUNCES) BUTTON
  MUSHROOMS

1 DRIED BAY LEAF

3 SPRIGS FRESH
  FLAT-LEAF PARSLEY

1 SPRIG FRESH THYME

1KG (2 POUNDS) GRAVY BEEF,
  CHOPPED COARSELY

150G (4½ OUNCES) SPECK,
  CHOPPED COARSELY

1 MEDIUM BROWN ONION
  (150G), CHOPPED FINELY

3 CLOVES GARLIC, CRUSHED

⅔ CUP (160ML) DRY RED WINE

¼ CUP (70G) TOMATO PASTE

12 BABY ONIONS (300G)

1 Heat 2 teaspoons of the oil in a 6-litre (24-cup) pressure cooker; cook mushrooms, stirring occasionally, for 3 minutes or until browned. Remove from cooker.

2 Tie bay leaf, parsley and thyme together with kitchen string to make a bouquet garni. Heat remaining oil in cooker; cook beef, in batches, until browned. Remove from cooker.

3 Cook speck in cooker until browned. Add chopped onion and garlic; cook, stirring, for 3 minutes or until onion softens. Return beef to cooker with wine, paste and bouquet garni; secure lid. Bring cooker to high pressure. Reduce heat to stabilise pressure; cook for 35 minutes.

4 Meanwhile, peel baby onions, leaving root ends intact.

5 Release pressure using the quick release method (see tips); remove lid. Add baby onions and mushrooms; secure lid. Bring cooker to high pressure. Reduce heat to stabilise pressure; cook 10 minutes. Release pressure using the quick release method; remove lid. Discard bouquet garni; season to taste.

tips *If you have an electric pressure cooker you won't need to reduce the heat to stabilise pressure, your cooker will automatically stabilise itself. Always check with the manufacturer's instructions before using. For the quick release method referred to, use tongs (steam can burn your fingers) to turn the pressure valve on top of the cooker to open the valve and release the steam (this releases the pressure quickly before you remove the lid).*

Recipe is not suitable to freeze.

serving suggestion *Serve with creamy mashed potatoes.*

CHINESE BRAISED OXTAIL

PREP + COOK TIME **40 MINUTES** SERVES **4**

1KG (2 POUNDS) BEEF OXTAIL, TRIMMED

½ CUP (125ML) JAPANESE SOY SAUCE

¼ CUP (60ML) CHINESE COOKING WINE (SHAO HSING)

¼ CUP (55G) FIRMLY PACKED DARK BROWN SUGAR

6 CLOVES GARLIC, BRUISED

12CM (4¾-INCH) PIECE FRESH GINGER (60G), PEELED, SLICED THICKLY

4 GREEN ONIONS (SCALLIONS), CHOPPED COARSELY

2 STAR ANISE

2 CINNAMON STICKS

3 X 5CM (2-INCH) STRIPS ORANGE RIND

½ CUP (125ML) WATER

2 GREEN ONIONS (SCALLIONS), SHREDDED FINELY

1 Cut oxtail into 4cm (1½-inch) pieces. Combine sauce, wine, sugar, garlic, ginger, chopped onion, star anise, cinnamon, rind and the water in a 6-litre (24-cup) pressure cooker; bring to the boil. Add oxtail; secure lid. Bring cooker to high pressure. Reduce heat to stabilise pressure; cook for 30 minutes.

2 Release pressure using the quick release method (see tips); remove lid. Transfer oxtail to a serving plate; drizzle with about ⅓ cup (80ml) of braising liquid. Sprinkle with shredded onion.

tips *If you have an electric pressure cooker you won't need to reduce the heat to stabilise pressure, your cooker will automatically stabilise itself. Always check with the manufacturer's instructions before using. For the quick release method referred to, use tongs (steam can burn your fingers) to turn the pressure valve on top of the cooker to open the valve and release the steam (this releases the pressure quickly before you remove the lid).*

Recipe is suitable to freeze for up to 3 months.

serving suggestion
Serve with steamed rice and asian greens.

SPICY LAMB IN TOMATO
& SPINACH SAUCE
(See recipe page 68)

photograph page 67

SPICY LAMB IN TOMATO & SPINACH SAUCE

PREP + COOK TIME **40 MINUTES** SERVES **4**

- 1 TABLESPOON VEGETABLE OIL
- 1KG (2-POUND) BONED LAMB LEG, CHOPPED COARSELY
- 1 MEDIUM BROWN ONION (150G), CHOPPED FINELY
- 3 CLOVES GARLIC, CRUSHED
- 2 FRESH SMALL RED THAI (SERRANO) CHILLIES, CHOPPED FINELY
- 2 TEASPOONS GROUND CORIANDER
- 2 TEASPOONS GARAM MASALA
- 1 TEASPOON GROUND CUMIN
- 1 TEASPOON GROUND FENUGREEK
- ½ TEASPOON GROUND TURMERIC
- 410G (13 OUNCES) CANNED CRUSHED TOMATOES
- ½ CUP (125ML) BEEF STOCK
- 100G (3 OUNCES) BABY SPINACH LEAVES, SHREDDED FINELY
- 2 TABLESPOONS FINELY CHOPPED FRESH CORIANDER (CILANTRO)

1 Heat half the oil in a 6-litre (24-cup) pressure cooker; cook lamb, in batches, until browned. Remove from cooker.

2 Heat remaining oil in cooker; cook onion, garlic and chilli, stirring, for 3 minutes or until onion softens. Add spices; cook, stirring, for 1 minute or until fragrant. Return lamb to cooker with tomatoes and stock; secure lid. Bring cooker to high pressure. Reduce heat to stabilise the pressure; cook for 25 minutes.

3 Release pressure using the quick release method (see tips); remove lid. Stir in spinach and coriander; season to taste.

tips *If you have an electric pressure cooker you won't need to reduce the heat to stabilise pressure, your cooker will automatically stabilise itself. Always check with the manufacturer's instructions before using. For the quick release method referred to, use tongs (steam can burn your fingers) to turn the pressure valve on top of the cooker to open the valve and release the steam (this releases the pressure quickly before you remove the lid).*

Recipe is suitable to freeze for up to 3 months.

serving suggestion *Serve with steamed basmati rice and warm naan.*

photograph page 70

HAM HOCK
WITH LENTILS

PREP + COOK TIME **35 MINUTES** SERVES **4**

- 1 HAM HOCK (1KG)
- 1 DRIED BAY LEAF
- 1 LITRE (4 CUPS) WATER
- 2 TABLESPOONS OLIVE OIL
- 1 LARGE BROWN ONION (200G), CHOPPED FINELY
- 2 CLOVES GARLIC, CRUSHED
- 2 TABLESPOONS TOMATO PASTE
- 1 MEDIUM CARROT (120G), CHOPPED COARSELY
- 1½ CUPS (300G) FRENCH-STYLE GREEN LENTILS
- ⅓ CUP COARSELY CHOPPED FRESH FLAT-LEAF PARSLEY

1 Combine ham, bay leaf and the water in a 6-litre (24-cup) pressure cooker; secure lid. Bring cooker to high pressure. Reduce heat to stabilise pressure; cook for 15 minutes.

2 Release pressure using the quick release method (see tips); remove lid. Strain mixture over a large heatproof bowl. Reserve ham and 3 cups (750ml) cooking liquid; discard bay leaf.

3 Heat oil in cooker; cook onion and garlic, stirring, for 3 minutes or until onion softens. Return ham to cooker with reserved cooking liquid, paste, carrot and lentils; secure lid. Bring cooker to high pressure. Reduce heat to stabilise pressure; cook for 15 minutes.

4 Release pressure using the quick release method (see tips); remove lid, season to taste. Remove ham from cooker. When cool enough to handle remove ham from bone, chop coarsely; discard skin, fat and bone.

5 Return ham to cooker, reheat before serving. Sprinkle with parsley.

tips If you have an electric pressure cooker you won't need to reduce the heat to stabilise pressure, your cooker will automatically stabilise itself. Always check with the manufacturer's instructions before using. For the quick release method referred to, use tongs (steam can burn your fingers) to turn the pressure valve on top of the cooker to open the valve and release the steam (this releases the pressure quickly before you remove the lid).

Recipe is not suitable to freeze.

HAM HOCK WITH LENTILS
(See recipe page 69)

ITALIAN CHILLI BRAISED PORK

PREP + COOK TIME **50 MINUTES** SERVES **4**

- 800G (1½-POUND) BONED PORK SHOULDER
- 2 TABLESPOONS OLIVE OIL
- 4 CLOVES GARLIC, CRUSHED
- 4 DRAINED ANCHOVY FILLETS, CHOPPED FINELY
- 410G (13 OUNCES) CANNED DICED TOMATOES
- ¼ CUP (60ML) WATER
- 2 TABLESPOONS FINELY CHOPPED FRESH OREGANO
- 1 TABLESPOON RINSED DRAINED BABY CAPERS
- ½ TEASPOON DRIED CHILLI FLAKES
- ½ CUP (75G) SEEDED KALAMATA OLIVES

1 Roll pork tightly; tie with kitchen string, at 2cm (¾-inch) intervals, to secure. Season pork. Heat half the oil in a 6-litre (24-cup) pressure cooker; cook pork until browned all over. Remove from cooker.

2 Heat remaining oil in cooker; cook garlic and anchovy, stirring, for 1 minute or until fragrant. Stir in tomatoes, the water, oregano, capers and chilli. Return pork to cooker; secure lid. Bring cooker to high pressure. Reduce heat to stabilise pressure; cook for 25 minutes.

3 Release pressure using the quick release method (see tips); remove lid. Remove pork, cover; stand 5 minutes then slice thinly. Stir olives into sauce; season to taste. Serve pork with sauce. Sprinkle with some extra oregano, if you like.

tips If you have an electric pressure cooker you won't need to reduce the heat to stabilise pressure, your cooker will automatically stabilise itself. Always check with the manufacturer's instructions before using. For the quick release method referred to, use tongs (steam can burn your fingers) to turn the pressure valve on top of the cooker to open the valve and release the steam (this releases the pressure quickly before you remove the lid).

If cooked slightly pink, pork is very tender and moist. If you prefer it well done, cook it for 2 minutes longer.

Recipe is not suitable to freeze.

serving suggestion
Serve with creamy polenta.

CARAMELISED
PEPPER PORK

PREP + COOK TIME **35 MINUTES** SERVES **4**

**3 SHALLOTS (75G),
CHOPPED FINELY**

2 CLOVES GARLIC, CRUSHED

2 TABLESPOONS FISH SAUCE

**1 TABLESPOON COARSELY
CRACKED BLACK PEPPER**

**800G (1½-POUND) BONELESS
PORK BELLY, RIND REMOVED,
CHOPPED COARSELY**

1 TABLESPOON PEANUT OIL

**2 TABLESPOONS
DARK BROWN SUGAR**

⅓ CUP (80ML) WATER

**2 GREEN ONIONS (SCALLIONS),
SLICED FINELY**

1 Combine shallot, garlic, sauce, pepper and pork in a large bowl.

2 Heat oil in a 6-litre (24-cup) pressure cooker; cook pork, in batches, until browned. Remove from cooker.

3 Return pork to cooker with sugar; cook, stirring, until sugar caramelises. Add the water; secure lid. Bring cooker to high pressure. Reduce heat to stabilise pressure; cook for 20 minutes.

4 Release pressure using the quick release method (see tips); remove lid. Serve sprinkled with green onion.

tips *If you have an electric pressure cooker you won't need to reduce the heat to stabilise pressure, your cooker will automatically stabilise itself. Always check with the manufacturer's instructions before using. For the quick release method referred to, use tongs (steam can burn your fingers) to turn the pressure valve on top of the cooker to open the valve and release the steam (this releases the pressure quickly before you remove the lid).*

Recipe is suitable to freeze for up to 3 months.

serving suggestion
Serve with steamed rice.

ONE-DISH DINNERS

PORK SAUSAGE
& ASPARAGUS FRITTATA

PREP + COOK TIME **40 MINUTES** SERVES **4**

**4 PORK AND FENNEL
SAUSAGES (300G)
1 TABLESPOON OLIVE OIL
1 LARGE SEBAGO POTATO
(300G), CUT INTO 2CM
(¾-INCH) PIECES
1 SMALL BROWN ONION (80G),
CHOPPED FINELY
1 CUP (250ML) WATER
6 EGGS, BEATEN LIGHTLY
½ CUP (125ML) MILK
¾ CUP (60G) FINELY
GRATED PARMESAN
130G (4 OUNCES)
ASPARAGUS, TRIMMED,
HALVED LENGTHWAYS
TOASTED BREAD, TO SERVE**

1 Squeeze the sausage meat from casings. Heat oil in a 26cm (10½-inch) (top measurement) 21cm (8½-inch) (base measurement) non-stick frying pan over medium heat; cook sausage meat, breaking it up into smaller pieces with a wooden spoon, until browned lightly. Remove from pan with a slotted spoon; drain on paper towel.

2 Add potato and onion to pan; cook, stirring occasionally, for 7 minutes or until onion is soft. Add the water; bring to the boil. Reduce heat; simmer, uncovered, for 8 minutes or until water is absorbed and potato is tender. Return sausage to pan.

3 Combine eggs, milk and ½ cup of the parmesan in a large jug or bowl; season well. Pour egg mixture into pan. Reduce heat to low; add asparagus, pushing into the egg mixture. Cook, covered, for 5 minutes or until almost set.

4 Preheat grill (broiler) on medium-high heat. Grill frittata for 2 minutes or until set and golden. (If the handle of the pan is not heatproof, wrap it in several layers of foil and keep it away from the direct heat.) Top frittata with remaining parmesan. Serve with toasted bread.

tips *Frittata can be made ahead of time and reheated until warm.*

Recipe is not suitable to freeze.

SPICED SALMON &
BROCCOLI PILAF

PREP + COOK TIME **35 MINUTES** SERVES **4**

1 TABLESPOON OLIVE OIL

1 MEDIUM BROWN ONION (150G), CHOPPED FINELY

2 CLOVES GARLIC, CRUSHED

1½ CUPS (300G) JASMINE RICE

3¼ CUPS (800ML) CHICKEN STOCK

1 TEASPOON GROUND CUMIN

1 TEASPOON GROUND CORIANDER

½ TEASPOON GROUND ALLSPICE

2 X 200G (6½-OUNCE) SKINLESS SALMON FILLETS

250G (8 OUNCES) BROCCOLI, CUT INTO SMALL FLORETS

⅓ CUP (55G) ROASTED ALMOND KERNELS, CHOPPED COARSELY

½ CUP LOOSELY PACKED FRESH CORIANDER (CILANTRO) LEAVES

1 MEDIUM LEMON (140G), CUT INTO CHEEKS

1 Heat oil in a large saucepan over medium heat; cook onion and garlic, stirring, for 5 minutes or until softened.

2 Add rice to pan; cook, stirring, for 2 minutes or until grains appear transparent. Stir in stock; bring to the boil. Reduce heat to low; simmer, covered, for 10 minutes.

3 Meanwhile, combine spices in a medium bowl, season; add salmon, toss to coat in spice mixture.

4 Place salmon and broccoli on rice; cook, covered, for a further 3 minutes. Remove pan from heat; stand for 5 minutes or until broccoli and rice are tender and stock is absorbed. Season to taste.

5 Remove salmon; flake into pieces. Use a fork to separate the rice grains. Top the pilaf with the flaked salmon, nuts and coriander. Serve with lemon cheeks.

tips Instead of broccoli, you can use a green vegetable of your choice, such as asparagus, spinach, peas, green beans or snow peas.

Recipe is not suitable to freeze.

CHICKEN & LEMON THYME
ONE-PAN PIE

PREP + COOK TIME **1 HOUR (+ COOLING)** SERVES **4**

750G (1½ POUNDS) CHICKEN THIGH FILLETS, SLICED THINLY

2 TABLESPOONS OLIVE OIL

1 MEDIUM LEEK (350G), SLICED THINLY

2 CLOVES GARLIC, CRUSHED

1 TABLESPOON FRESH LEMON THYME LEAVES

½ CUP (70G) SLIVERED ALMONDS

¼ CUP (35G) PLAIN (ALL-PURPOSE) FLOUR

3 CUPS (750ML) CHICKEN STOCK

445G (14-OUNCE) SHEET SOUR CREAM SHORTCRUST PASTRY OR 2 SHEETS PUFF PASTRY

1 EGG, BEATEN LIGHTLY

1 Preheat oven to 200°C/400°F.

2 Season chicken. Heat oil in a 25cm (10-inch) (top measurement) 19cm (7¾-inch) (base measurement) large ovenproof frying pan over high heat; cook chicken, in batches, stirring occasionally, for 3 minutes or until browned. Remove from pan.

3 Add leek to same pan; cook, stirring occasionally, for 3 minutes or until softened. Add garlic, thyme and almonds; cook, stirring, for 1 minute or until fragrant. Return chicken to pan with flour; cook, stirring, for 1 minute. Gradually stir in stock; bring to the boil. Reduce heat to medium-low; simmer, uncovered, stirring occasionally, for 5 minutes or until thickened slightly. Season to taste; cool for 10 minutes.

4 Trim pastry to fit top of pan. Cut pastry off-cuts into decorative shapes. Top pie with pastry shapes; brush with egg.

5 Bake pie for 20 minutes or until pastry is golden.

tips *The filling can be made, covered and refrigerated, up to 2 days ahead.*

This recipe is suitable to freeze for 3 months if made in an ovenproof dish.

CHEESY SMOKED BAKED BEANS WITH PUMPKIN

PREP + COOK TIME **45 MINUTES** SERVES **4**

- ½ CUP (125ML) EXTRA VIRGIN OLIVE OIL
- 1 MEDIUM RED ONION (170G), CUT INTO WEDGES
- 350G (11 OUNCES) JAP PUMPKIN, CHOPPED
- 3 X 400G (12½-OUNCE) CANS FOUR-BEAN MIX, DRAINED, RINSED
- 400G (12½ OUNCES) CANNED CHICKPEAS (GARBANZO BEANS), DRAINED, RINSED
- 1 CHIPOTLE CHILLI IN ADOBO SAUCE, CHOPPED FINELY
- ¼ CUP (50G) ADOBO SAUCE FROM CANNED CHIPOTLE CHILLI IN ADOBO SAUCE
- 1 TABLESPOON HONEY
- 2 TABLESPOONS BARBECUE SAUCE
- 1 TEASPOON DIJON MUSTARD
- 700G (1½ POUNDS) BOTTLED TOMATO PASSATA
- ¾ CUP (90G) COARSELY GRATED CHEDDAR
- ⅓ CUP (40G) COARSELY GRATED SMOKED CHEDDAR
- 2 CLOVES GARLIC, CRUSHED
- 4 X 110G (3½ OUNCES) CIABATTA ROLLS, HALVED

1 Preheat oven to 220°C/425°F.

2 Heat 2 tablespoons of the oil in a large ovenproof frying pan over high heat; cook onion and pumpkin, stirring occasionally, for 4 minutes or until onion has softened slightly. Add beans, chickpeas, chilli, adobo sauce, honey, barbecue sauce and mustard; cook, stirring occasionally, for 3 minutes or until heated through. Stir in passata; bring to the boil. Boil, uncovered, for 3 minutes or until thickened slightly; season to taste.

3 Sprinkle bean mixture with cheeses. Bake for 15 minutes or until cheese is browned lightly.

4 Meanwhile, combine garlic and remaining oil in a small bowl; season. Brush garlic mixture over cut side of rolls. Place rolls on an oven tray; bake on separate shelf with beans for 6 minutes or until golden.

5 Serve baked beans with torn garlic bread.

tips You can use potatoes or kumara (orange sweet potato) instead of pumpkin in this recipe if you like.

Chipotle chilli with adobo sauce can be found in most good grocers and delicatessens.

Recipe is not suitable to freeze.

GARLIC & SAGE
PORK CUTLETS WITH PEARS

PREP + COOK TIME **45 MINUTES** SERVES **4**

4 MEDIUM PEARS (920G)

2 CLOVES GARLIC, CRUSHED

14 MEDIUM FRESH SAGE LEAVES

⅓ CUP (80ML) OLIVE OIL

4 X 200G (6½-OUNCE) PORK CUTLETS WITH RIND, RIND SCORED IN 5MM (¼-INCH) SLICES

⅓ CUP (80ML) DRY SHERRY

1KG (2 POUNDS) BABY DESIREE POTATOES, HALVED LENGTHWAYS

40G (1½ OUNCES) MIXED BABY SALAD LEAVES

2 TEASPOONS LEMON JUICE

1 Preheat oven to 200°C/400°F.

2 Halve and quarter pears.

3 Using a mortar and pestle, pound garlic and 6 sage leaves to a paste. Stir in half the oil; season to taste. Rub mixture over pork.

4 Heat remaining oil in a large ovenproof frying pan over high heat; cook pork, skin-side down, for 2 minutes or until crisp. Cook pork a further 1 minute on each side or until browned. Transfer to a plate.

5 Cook remaining sage in same pan for 30 seconds or until crisp; drain on paper towel.

6 Add 1 tablespoon sherry to same pan; cook, scraping the sediments off base of pan with a wooden spoon. Reduce heat to medium. Add pear; cook for 2 minutes each side or until golden. Add remaining sherry and potato; stir for 1 minute or until potato is coated.

7 Transfer pan to oven; roast for 10 minutes or until pears are cooked. Remove pears; cover to keep warm. Add pork to pan; roast pork and potato mixture for a further 10 minutes or until potato is tender and pork is just cooked through. Season to taste.

8 Combine salad leaves and juice in a medium bowl; season to taste.

9 Serve potato and pears topped with pork, sage leaves and salad mixture.

tips *You can substitute baby desiree with kipfler (fingerling) potatoes, if you like.*

Recipe is not suitable to freeze.

SMOKED PORK SAUSAGE
& KIPFLER GOULASH

(See recipe page 90)

photograph page 89

SMOKED PORK
SAUSAGE &
KIPFLER GOULASH

PREP + COOK TIME **45 MINUTES** SERVES **4**

2 TABLESPOONS OLIVE OIL

500G (1 POUND) GOOD-QUALITY PORK SAUSAGES

2 SMALL RED ONIONS (200G), CUT INTO WEDGES

500G (1 POUND) SMALL KIPFLER (FINGERLING) POTATOES, SCRUBBED, HALVED LENGTHWAYS

2 CLOVES GARLIC, CRUSHED

2 TABLESPOONS TOMATO PASTE

2¼ TEASPOONS SMOKED PAPRIKA

½ TEASPOON FENNEL SEEDS

400G (12½ OUNCES) CANNED CRUSHED TOMATOES

1 CUP (250ML) CHICKEN STOCK

⅓ CUP (80G) SOUR CREAM

½ CUP (55G) COARSELY CHOPPED WALNUTS, TOASTED

BABY PARSLEY LEAVES, TO SERVE

1 Heat oil in a large frying pan over high heat. Squeeze pieces of sausage out of skins into pan; cook, stirring occasionally, for 5 minutes or until golden brown. Remove from pan with a slotted spoon; drain on paper towel.

2 Add onion and potato to same pan; cook, stirring occasionally, for 5 minutes or until onion has softened. Return sausage to pan with garlic, paste, 2 teaspoons of the paprika and seeds; cook, stirring, for 2 minutes or until fragrant. Add tomatoes and stock; bring to the boil. Reduce heat to medium; simmer, covered, for 20 minutes or until potato is tender and sauce reduces slightly. Season to taste.

3 Serve goulash topped with sour cream, nuts, remaining paprika and parsley.

tips Goulash can be made up until the end of step 2, covered and refrigerated, up to 2 days ahead.

Recipe is not suitable to freeze.

photograph page 92

LAMB & MINT
MEATBALLS
WITH RISONI

PREP + COOK TIME **50 MINUTES** SERVES **4**

- 500G (1 POUND) MINCED (GROUND) LAMB
- 1 CUP (70G) STALE BREADCRUMBS
- ¼ CUP CHOPPED FRESH MINT LEAVES
- 1 EGG, BEATEN LIGHTLY
- 1 MEDIUM BROWN ONION (150G), GRATED
- 2 CLOVES GARLIC, CRUSHED
- ¼ CUP (60ML) OLIVE OIL
- 1 LARGE EGGPLANT (500G), CUT INTO 3CM (1¼-INCH) CUBES
- 1½ CUPS (330G) RISONI PASTA
- 2⅔ CUPS (680G) BOTTLED TOMATO PASSATA
- 1½ CUPS (375ML) CHICKEN STOCK
- 125G (4 OUNCES) GREEK FETTA, CRUMBLED
- 2 TABLESPOONS FRESH SMALL MINT LEAVES, EXTRA

1 Combine lamb, breadcrumbs, chopped mint, egg, onion and garlic in a medium bowl; season well. Roll ¼ cup measures of mixture into balls.

2 Heat half the oil in a large frying pan; cook meatballs, shaking pan occasionally, until browned all over. Remove from pan with a slotted spoon.

3 Heat remaining oil in same pan over medium-high heat; cook eggplant for 4 minutes or until golden brown.

4 Return meatballs to pan with risoni, passata and stock; stir to combine. Bring to the boil. Reduce heat to low; simmer, covered, stirring occasionally, for 15 minutes or until the risoni is tender.

5 Serve meatball mixture topped with fetta and extra mint leaves.

tips Uncooked meatballs can be frozen for up to 3 months.

If risoni mixture is too thick, add a little boiling water to moisten. Mixture will thicken on standing.

LAMB & MINT MEATBALLS
WITH RISONI
(See recipe page 91)

PRAWN
JAMBALAYA

PREP + COOK TIME **55 MINUTES (+ STANDING)** SERVES **4**

2 TABLESPOONS OLIVE OIL

4 CHICKEN THIGHS CUTLETS
(800G)

250G (8 OUNCES) CURED
CHORIZO SAUSAGE, SLICED

2 MEDIUM BROWN ONIONS
(300G), CHOPPED

3 CLOVES GARLIC, CRUSHED

2 CELERY STALKS (300G),
TRIMMED, SLICED

1 TABLESPOON CAJUN
SEASONING

2 TEASPOONS SWEET PAPRIKA

1 MEDIUM RED CAPSICUM
(BELL PEPPER) (200G),
CHOPPED

1 MEDIUM GREEN CAPSICUM
(BELL PEPPER) (200G),
CHOPPED

400G (12½ OUNCES) CANNED
DICED TOMATOES

2 CUPS (500ML) CHICKEN
STOCK

1½ CUPS (300G) LONG GRAIN
WHITE RICE

8 LARGE UNCOOKED PRAWNS
(SHRIMP) (560G)

¼ CUP COARSELY CHOPPED
FRESH FLAT-LEAF PARSLEY

1 MEDIUM LEMON (140G),
CUT INTO WEDGES

1 Heat oil in a large saucepan over medium heat; cook chicken for 10 minutes or until browned well all over. Remove from pan; cover to keep warm.

2 Add chorizo, onion, garlic, celery, cajun seasoning and paprika to same pan; cook, stirring occasionally, for 10 minutes or until vegetables are softened. Stir in capsicum.

3 Return chicken to pan with tomatoes and stock; bring to the boil. Reduce heat; simmer, covered, for 10 minutes or until capsicum is tender. Add rice; cook, covered, for 12 minutes.

4 Meanwhile, shell and devein prawns, leaving tails intact.

5 Add prawns to pan; cook, covered, for a further 3 minutes or until prawns are just cooked through. Remove from heat; stand for 5 minutes. Fluff rice with a fork; season to taste. Stir in parsley; serve with lemon wedges.

tips You can leave out the prawns for a chicken version, if preferred.

Coriander (cilantro) could be used in place of the parsley.

Recipe is not suitable to freeze.

VEAL & CREAMY
MUSHROOM
SAUCE

PREP + COOK TIME **45 MINUTES** SERVES **4**

60G (2 OUNCES) BUTTER

400G (12½ OUNCES) VEAL FILLET, SLICED THINLY

3 SHALLOTS (75G), HALVED

200G (6½ OUNCES) SWISS BROWN MUSHROOMS, SLICED

500G (1 POUND) KIPFLER (FINGERLING) POTATOES, CUT INTO 1CM (½-INCH) ROUNDS

⅓ CUP (80ML) DRY WHITE WINE

1 CUP (250ML) CHICKEN STOCK

1 TABLESPOON WORCESTERSHIRE SAUCE

2 TEASPOONS DIJON MUSTARD

250G (8 OUNCES) CRÈME FRAÎCHE

¼ CUP CHOPPED FRESH CHIVES

50G (1½ OUNCES) BABY SPINACH LEAVES

1 Melt one-third of the butter in a large non-stick frying pan over high heat; cook veal for 1 minute each side or until browned lightly. Transfer to a plate, cover to keep warm.

2 Heat half the remaining butter in same pan, add shallot and mushroom; cook, stirring, for 5 minutes or until liquid has evaporated. Remove from pan.

3 Melt remaining butter in same pan, add potato; cook, stirring, for 10 minutes or until lightly browned and tender. Remove from the pan.

4 Add wine to pan, cook, stirring, for 1 minute or until reduced slightly. Add stock, sauce and mustard; bring to the boil. Reduce heat to medium-low; simmer, uncovered, for 3 minutes or until reduced by half. Whisk in crème fraîche and half the chives.

5 Return potato, mushroom and veal to pan to warm through. Stir in spinach. Serve topped with remaining chives.

tips *Swiss brown mushrooms have a stronger flavour than button mushrooms, which can be used instead, if you prefer.*

Recipe is not suitable to freeze.

serving suggestion *Serve with a crisp garden salad.*

CHICKEN
IN TURMERIC
& YOGHURT

PREP + COOK TIME **45 MINUTES** SERVES **4**

- 2 TABLESPOONS EXTRA VIRGIN OLIVE OIL
- 4 CHICKEN THIGH CUTLETS (800G)
- 4 CHICKEN DRUMSTICKS (600G)
- 2 MEDIUM ONIONS (300G), SLICED THINLY
- 4 CLOVES GARLIC, CRUSHED
- 1 TEASPOON GROUND TURMERIC
- 2 TEASPOONS CUMIN SEEDS
- ½ CUP (140G) GREEK-STYLE YOGHURT, PLUS EXTRA TO SERVE
- ½ CUP (125ML) CHICKEN STOCK
- 2 LONG FRESH RED CHILLIES
- 2 LONG FRESH GREEN CHILIES
- 500G (1 POUND) CAULIFLOWER, CUT INTO FLORETS
- ½ CUP (100G) COUSCOUS
- ½ SMALL RED ONION (50G), SLICED THINLY
- 1 TABLESPOON WHITE BALSAMIC VINEGAR
- ¼ CUP LOOSELY PACKED FRESH CORIANDER (CILANTRO) LEAVES

1 Heat oil in a large deep frying pan over medium heat; cook chicken, in batches, for 10 minutes or until browned all over. Remove from pan.

2 Add onion, garlic and spices to same pan; cook, stirring, for 5 minutes or until soft. Stir in yoghurt and stock.

3 Return chicken to pan, bring to a simmer. Reduce heat; simmer, covered, for 10 minutes.

4 Meanwhile, chop one red and one green chilli and leave remaining whole. Add whole chillies and cauliflower to pan; cook, covered, for 5 minutes or until cauliflower is tender. Remove pan from heat. Remove chicken, cauliflower and ½ cup liquid from pan; keep warm. Add couscous to centre of pan; cover with a lid. Stand for 5 minutes or until liquid is absorbed. Fluff couscous with a fork; season to taste. Return chicken and cauliflower to pan and drizzle with reserved sauce.

5 Combine onion and balsamic in a small bowl; stand for 10 mintues.

6 Top chicken mixture with onion, chopped chilli and coriander. Serve with extra yoghurt.

tips For a gluten-free version, leave out the couscous and serve with steamed rice, drizzled with the pan juices.

Recipe is not suitable to freeze.

SLOW
COMFORT

ROASTS
& BAKES

CONFIT DUCK & CANDIED ORANGE SALAD

PREP + COOK TIME **4 HOURS (+ REFRIGERATION)** SERVES **4**

1 TABLESPOON THYME LEAVES

⅓ CUP (100G) COARSE COOKING SALT (KOSHER SALT)

2 TABLESPOONS CHINESE FIVE-SPICE POWDER

4 DUCK MARYLANDS (1.2KG)

2 CLOVES GARLIC, BRUISED

2 LITRES (8 CUPS) OLIVE OIL, APPROXIMATELY

⅓ CUP (75G) CASTER (SUPERFINE) SUGAR

⅓ CUP (80ML) WATER

3 WHOLE CLOVES

1 MEDIUM ORANGE (240G), SLICED THINLY

120G (4 OUNCES) BABY ROCKET (ARUGULA) LEAVES

1 CUP LOOSELY PACKED CHERVIL SPRIGS

⅓ CUP (35G) WALNUT HALVES, ROASTED

VERJUICE DRESSING

1 TEASPOON DIJON MUSTARD

1 TABLESPOON VERJUICE

1½ TABLESPOONS OLIVE OIL

1 Combine thyme, salt and five-spice in a small bowl. Place duck in a shallow dish; rub salt mixture all over duck. Cover; refrigerate for 2 hours.

2 Preheat oven to 130°C/260°F.

3 Wash salt mixture from duck; pat duck dry with paper towel. Place duck and garlic, tightly packed in a single layer, in a medium ovenproof dish. Pour in enough oil to completely cover duck. Cook duck in the oven for 3 hours or until very tender.

4 Meanwhile, stir sugar, the water and cloves in a large frying pan, over medium heat, without boiling, until sugar dissolves. Add orange slices; bring to the boil. Reduce heat; simmer, uncovered, swirling the pan occasionally, for 1 hour or until liquid has nearly evaporated and oranges are sticky.

5 Make verjuice dressing.

6 Carefully remove duck from oil. Heat 2 tablespoons of the confit cooking oil in a large frying pan over high heat. Cook duck for 2 minutes each side, or until golden. Remove from heat. When cool enough to handle, remove meat from bones; discard bones, shred meat and skin coarsely.

7 Place duck, orange and dressing in a large bowl with remaining ingredients; toss gently to combine.

verjuice dressing Place ingredients in a screw-top jar; shake well. Season to taste.

tips Duck can be cooked up to 4 days ahead. Keep covered in oil in the fridge. To reheat duck, remove from oil, place on an oven tray and cook under a preheated grill for 10 minutes or until skin is crisp and heated through.

Recipe is not suitable to freeze.

TEA-BRINED
ROASTEDCHICKEN

PREP + COOK TIME **1½ HOURS (+ REFRIGERATION)** SERVES **4**

You will need to start this recipe the day before.

1 LITRE (4 CUPS) WATER
½ CUP (30G) RUSSIAN CARAVAN TEA LEAVES
½ CUP (175G) HONEY
½ CUP (110G) WHITE (GRANULATED) SUGAR
2 LEMONS (1 SLICED, 1 WHOLE)
⅓ CUP (40G) SEA SALT FLAKES
1 BUNCH FRESH SAGE
1.8KG (3½ POUND) WHOLE CHICKEN
1 TABLESPOON OLIVE OIL

1 Place the water and tea leaves in a saucepan over high heat; bring to the boil. Remove from the heat; stand until cooled completely. Strain; discard leaves.
2 Stir the honey, sugar, sliced lemon and salt flakes through the tea mixture until well combined.
3 Place a large sealable bag in a large bowl; add half the sage, then the chicken, breast-side down. Carefully pour the tea mixture over the chicken and seal the bag, removing all the air. Refrigerate for 8 hours or overnight, rotating three times.
4 Preheat oven to 180°C/350°F.
5 Remove chicken from brine (discard brine); pat dry with paper towel. Place in a large roasting pan. Place remaining sage and the whole lemon in the chicken cavity; truss the legs with kitchen string. Drizzle over olive oil and season with salt and pepper. Roast for 1¼ hours or until the juices run clear when the thickest part of a thigh is pierced. (Cover the parts of the chicken that brown faster with foil.)

tips *Russian caravan tea is a blend of China black keemun, oolong and lapsang souchong teas. It's not actually from Russia, but was transported to Russia from China. It is the lapsang souchong that gives the tea its defining smoky flavour. It is available from select supermarkets and tea shops.*

Recipe is not suitable to freeze.

serving suggestion *Serve with roasted mixed heirloom carrots and potatoes.*

LEMON THYME CHICKEN WITH
CAPERBERRY
SALSA

PREP + COOK TIME **50 MINUTES (+ STANDING)** SERVES **4**

4 FREE-RANGE CHICKEN BREAST SUPREME (1KG) (SEE TIPS)
¼ CUP (60ML) OLIVE OIL
2 TABLESPOONS FRESH THYME LEAVES
1 TABLESPOON FINELY GRATED LEMON RIND
1 CELERIAC (CELERY ROOT) (750G), PEELED
2 LARGE CARROTS (360G)
1 CLOVE GARLIC, CRUSHED
2 TABLESPOONS WHITE BALSAMIC VINEGAR
½ CUP (100G) ROASTED PEPITAS (PUMPKIN SEEDS)
¾ CUP COARSELY CHOPPED FRESH FLAT-LEAF PARSLEY
2 TABLESPOONS GREEK-STYLE YOGHURT
¼ CUP FRESH FLAT-LEAF PARSLEY LEAVES, EXTRA
¼ CUP FRESH THYME SPRIGS, EXTRA

CAPERBERRY SALSA
1 CUP (160G) CAPERBERRIES
2 TABLESPOONS OLIVE OIL
2 TABLESPOONS LEMON JUICE
1½ TEASPOONS DRIED PINK PEPPERCORNS, CRUSHED COARSELY

1 Preheat oven to 220°C/425°F. Line an oven tray with baking paper.

2 Combine chicken, 1 tablespoon oil, thyme and rind in a large bowl; stand for 10 minutes.

3 Meanwhile, using a vegetable peeler, peel long thin ribbons from the celeriac and carrot (keep the centre core of each vegetable for another use, see tips). Place vegetable ribbons in a large bowl with garlic, vinegar, pepitas, chopped parsley and yoghurt; season. Stir to combine.

4 Heat a large frying pan over medium-high heat; cook chicken for 3 minutes each side or until browned all over. Transfer to tray; roast for 12 minutes or until cooked through.

5 Meanwhile, make caperberry salsa.

6 Serve chicken with vegetable salad and caperberry salsa; top with extra herbs.

caperberry salsa Halve three-quarters of the caperberries, keeping the stems attached; reserve remaining for serving. Combine halved caperberries in a small bowl with oil, juice and peppercorns.

tips Chicken breast supreme is a chicken breast with the skin and wing bone attached. Ask your butcher to prepare it for you or use skinless chicken breast fillets instead.

You can use the remaining centre core of the celeriac and carrot in a soup.

Recipe is not suitable to freeze.

PORT SMOKED
BEEF

PREP + COOK TIME **1¼ HOURS (+ REFRIGERATION & STANDING)**
SERVES **8**

You will need to start this recipe the day before.

EQUIPMENT
**1 CUP (125G) HANDFUL
  SMOKING WOOD CHIPS**
BARBECUE SMOKER BOX

PORT-SMOKED BEEF
2 TABLESPOONS OLIVE OIL
2 CLOVES GARLIC, CRUSHED
¼ CUP (60ML) PORT
**2 TABLESPOONS COARSELY
  CHOPPED FRESH OREGANO**
**1.5KG (3-POUND) PIECE BEEF
  EYE FILLET, TRIMMED**
1 CUP (250ML) PORT, EXTRA

1 Combine oil, garlic, port and oregano in a large bowl; add beef, turn to coat in marinade. Cover; refrigerate overnight.
2 Meanwhile, combine smoking chips and extra port in a small bowl. Cover; stand overnight.
3 Cook beef, uncovered, on a heated oiled barbecue until just browned all over. Place beef in a lightly oiled, deep, doubled disposable aluminium roasting tray. Place drained smoking chips in a smoker box; place alongside beef on the barbecue.
4 Cook beef, in covered barbecue, at 180°C/350°F for 45 minutes for medium or until cooked as desired. Remove beef from barbecue, cover; rest for 10 minutes before carving.

tips Different smoking chips add different flavours to meat, but not in the way you might necessarily expect. The aroma of the wood doesn't actually carry through to the meat, rather it is the way in which wood burns, which in turn affects the amount of smoke it produces. Ultimately, the smoke flavour should enhance the meat rather than mask the taste.

Recipe is not suitable to freeze.

***serving suggestion** Serve with roasted jap pumpkin wedges, and accompany with aioli or your favourite relish or chutney.*

ROAST VEAL RACK
WITH CELERIAC &
POTATO GRATIN

PREP + COOK TIME **1 HOUR 50 MINUTES** SERVES **8**

2KG (4-POUND) VEAL RACK (8 CUTLETS)
1 CUP (250ML) WATER
¼ CUP (70G) DIJON MUSTARD
2 TABLESPOONS HORSERADISH CREAM
2 CLOVES GARLIC, CRUSHED
1½ TABLESPOONS PLAIN (ALL-PURPOSE) FLOUR
2 TEASPOONS WHOLEGRAIN MUSTARD
2 CUPS (500ML) BEEF STOCK
2 TABLESPOONS FINELY CHOPPED TARRAGON
1 TABLESPOON COARSELY CHOPPED FRESH THYME
¼ CUP FINELY CHOPPED FRESH FLAT-LEAF PARSLEY

CELERIAC & POTATO GRATIN
600ML THICKENED (HEAVY) CREAM
3 CLOVES GARLIC, SLICED THINLY
3 TEASPOONS CHOPPED FRESH THYME LEAVES
1 MEDIUM CELERIAC (CELERY ROOT) (750G), TRIMMED
3 MEDIUM POTATOES (600G)

50G (1½ OUNCES) SMOKED CHEDDAR, GRATED COARSELY
1 TEASPOON FRESH THYME, EXTRA

1 Preheat oven to 180°C/350°F.
2 Make celeriac and potato gratin.
3 Meanwhile, place veal on a wire rack in a flameproof roasting pan; pour the water into the base of the pan. Combine dijon mustard, horseradish and garlic in a small bowl. Spread mustard mixture over veal; season. Roast veal for last 45 minutes of gratin cooking time or until cooked as desired. Transfer veal to a plate. Cover; rest for 10 minutes.
4 Heat roasting pan over medium-high heat, add flour; cook, whisking, until mixture is smooth and bubbly. Add wholegrain mustard and stock; stir until mixture boils and thickens. Season to taste.
5 Combine herbs; press onto veal. Cut veal into cutlets; serve with gratin and mustard sauce.

celeriac & potato gratin Place cream, garlic and thyme in a medium saucepan over medium heat; bring to a simmer. Remove from heat; stand for 10 minutes. Meanwhile, using a mandoline or V-slicer, thinly slice celeriac and potatoes; combine in a large bowl. Layer celeriac and potato with cream mixture and salt and pepper in a 1.5-litre (6-cup) round ovenproof dish. Sprinkle with cheese. Cover with foil; bake for 1 hour. Uncover, bake for 20 minutes or until tender and golden. Top with extra thyme.

tip Recipe is not suitable to freeze.

serving suggestion Serve with roman or green beans.

SLOW-ROASTED LAMB SHOULDER
(See recipe page 116)

photograph page 115

SLOW-ROASTED
LAMB SHOULDER

PREP + COOK TIME **3¾ HOURS** SERVES **4**

1.3KG (2¾-POUND) LAMB SHOULDER, SHANK ON

2 TABLESPOONS OLIVE OIL

1KG (2 POUNDS) POTATOES, SLICED THICKLY

2 MEDIUM ONIONS (300G), SLICED THINLY

4 DRAINED ANCHOVY FILLETS, CHOPPED FINELY

2 RED GARLIC BULBS (140G)

1 MEDIUM LEMON (140G), CUT INTO WEDGES

3 SPRIGS FRESH ROSEMARY

1 CUP (250ML) CHICKEN STOCK

1 CUP (250ML) WATER OR DRY WHITE WINE

1 Preheat oven to 180°C/350°F. Season lamb.

2 Heat a flameproof roasting pan over a medium high heat. Add oil, then lamb; cook until lamb is well browned all over. Remove from pan.

3 Layer potato, onion and anchovies in roasting pan; season between layers. Cut garlic bulbs in half horizontally; place on vegetables with lemon wedges.

4 Place lamb on top of vegetable mixture; add rosemary. Pour combined stock and the water over vegetables. Cover pan tightly with two layers of foil. Roast for 1½ hours. Remove foil, reduce oven to 160°C/325°F; roast for a further 1½ hours or until the meat can be pulled from the bone easily. Transfer lamb to a tray. Cover with foil; rest 20 minutes. Increase oven to 200°C/400°F.

5 Meanwhile, return vegetable mixture in pan to oven; cook for a further 20 minutes or until browned.

6 Serve lamb with vegetables, garlic and lemon.

tips *This recipe is best made close to serving.*

Recipe is not suitable to freeze.

serving suggestion *Serve with a green salad or Greek salad and lemon wedges.*

photograph page 118

MEATLOAF WITH
FIG GLAZE

PREP + COOK TIME **1½ HOURS** SERVES **6**

2 SLICES WHITE BREAD (90G)

½ CUP (125ML) MILK

1 TABLESPOON OLIVE OIL

1 MEDIUM CARROT (120G), CHOPPED FINELY

1 TRIMMED CELERY STICK (100G), CHOPPED FINELY

3 SHALLOTS (75G), CHOPPED FINELY

2 CLOVES GARLIC, CRUSHED

1KG (2 POUNDS) MINCED (GROUND) PORK AND VEAL (SEE TIPS)

1 TABLESPOON FINELY CHOPPED FRESH MARJORAM LEAVES

⅓ CUP (110G) FIG JAM

½ CUP (115G) GLACÉ GINGER

1 TABLESPOON BOILING WATER

CARAMELISED SHALLOTS

30G (1 OUNCE) BUTTER

8 SHALLOTS (200G), HALVED

¼ CUP (60ML) DRY RED WINE

6 FRESH BAY LEAVES

1 Preheat oven to 200°C/400°F. Line a large oven tray with baking paper.

2 Place bread and milk in a large bowl; stand for 10 minutes or until milk is absorbed.

3 Meanwhile, heat oil in a large saucepan over medium-high heat; cook carrot, celery, shallots and garlic for 5 minutes or until soft.

4 Add carrot mixture to bread mixture with pork and veal, and marjoram; season well. Mix well.

5 Shape meatloaf mixture into a 20cm (8-inch) log in the centre of a 40cm (16-inch) piece of baking paper. Using the baking paper as a guide, roll to form a 30cm (12-inch) log. Transfer meatloaf on paper to oven tray.

6 Process jam, ginger and water until smooth; brush over meatloaf.

7 Bake meatloaf for 45 minutes or until cooked through and browned.

8 Meanwhile, make caramelised shallots.

9 Serve meatloaf topped with shallots.

caramelised shallots Melt butter in a small ovenproof frying pan over medium heat; cook shallots, stirring, 5 minutes or until softened slightly. Add wine; bring to the boil. Transfer pan to the oven; cook for 15 minutes. Add bay leaves; cook for a further 5 minutes or until shallots are tender and caramelised.

tips *Some butchers sell a pork and veal mince mixture. If it is not available as a mixture, buy 500g (1 pound) of each.*

If you don't have an ovenproof frying pan, use a flameproof baking dish or transfer the shallot mixture from the frying pan to an ovenproof dish.

Recipe is not suitable to freeze.

serving suggestion *Serve with mashed potato.*

**MEATLOAF
WITH FIG GLAZE**

(See recipe page 117)

CIDER-ROASTED
PORK BELLY

PREP + COOK TIME **3 HOURS** SERVES **4**

1.5KG (3-POUND) PIECE PORK
  BELLY, RIND ON
2 TABLESPOONS FINELY
  CHOPPED FRESH ROSEMARY
1 TABLESPOON
  SEA SALT FLAKES
1⅓ CUPS (330ML) APPLE CIDER
4 MEDIUM PARSNIPS (1KG),
  PEELED, CUT INTO
  QUARTERS
4 CLOVES GARLIC, PEELED
1½ CUPS (375ML) SALT-
  REDUCED CHICKEN OR
  VEGETABLE STOCK
2 MEDIUM GREEN-SKINNED
  APPLES (300G)
800G (1½ POUNDS)
  CANNED BROWN LENTILS,
  DRAINED, RINSED

1 Preheat oven to 240°C/475°F.
2 Using a sharp knife, score pork rind at 1cm (½-inch) intervals in a criss-cross pattern. Place pork, rind-side up, in a large roasting pan. Combine rosemary and salt in a small bowl; rub salt mixture over pork. Roast pork, uncovered, for 20 minutes or until rind starts to blister and crackle.
3 Reduce oven to 160°C/325°F. Add cider to pan; roast for 1¼ hours.
4 Add parsnips, garlic and stock to pan; roast, uncovered, for 45 minutes.
5 Cut unpeeled apples into quarters, add to pan with lentils; roast for a further 30 minutes or until apple is tender. Season mixture to taste.
6 Serve sliced pork with apple mixture.

tips To make crisp crackling, the pork rind needs to be really dry: leave the pork rind uncovered in the fridge overnight; cover the pork flesh with plastic wrap to stop it from drying out.

Recipe is not suitable to freeze.

serving suggestion
Serve with a green salad.

ROAST PORK WITH APPLE SAUCE

PREP + COOK TIME **1½ HOURS** SERVES **6**

6-POINT RACK OF PORK (1.6KG), RIND SCORED
1 TABLESPOON OLIVE OIL
1 TABLESPOON COARSE COOKING SALT (KOSHER SALT)
2 TEASPOONS FENNEL SEEDS, CRUSHED

APPLE SAUCE
3 LARGE GRANNY SMITH APPLES (600G), PEELED, CORED, SLICED THICKLY
½ CUP (125ML) WATER
1 TEASPOON CASTER (SUPERFINE) SUGAR
¼ TEASPOON GROUND CINNAMON

1 Preheat oven to 250°C/480°F.

2 Pat the pork dry with paper towel. Place the pork on a rack in a roasting pan. Rub the rind with the oil, then the combined salt and crushed fennel seeds.

3 Roast pork for 40 minutes or until the skin blisters. Reduce oven to 180°C/350°F; roast for a further 35 minutes or until pork is just cooked. To test if pork is cooked, insert a meat thermometer into a middle section of the meat; it should register 62°C/145°F. Alternatively, insert a metal skewer; the juices should run clear.

4 Meanwhile, make apple sauce.

5 Serve pork with apple sauce.

apple sauce Place apple and the water in a medium saucepan; simmer, uncovered, for 15 minutes or until apple is soft. Stir in sugar and cinnamon.

tips Crush the fennel seeds in a mortar and pestle if you have one, otherwise you can chop them with a knife.

To make crisp crackling, the pork rind needs to be really dry: leave the pork rind uncovered in the fridge overnight; cover the pork flesh with plastic wrap to stop it from drying out.

Recipe is not suitable to freeze.

serving suggestion Serve with seasonal vegetables such as roast potatoes, brussels sprouts or celeriac.

ROASTED SNAPPER WITH HORSERADISH MAYO

PREP + COOK TIME **50 MINUTES** SERVES **2**

- 400G (12½ OUNCES) POTATOES
- 6 CLOVES GARLIC
- 2 TABLESPOONS OLIVE OIL
- 2 WHOLE BABY SNAPPER (600G)
- 1 MEDIUM LEMON (140G), SLICED THINLY
- ⅓ CUP LOOSELY PACKED FRESH DILL SPRIGS
- ¼ CUP (75G) MAYONNAISE
- 2 TEASPOONS HORSERADISH CREAM
- 2 TEASPOONS DRAINED CAPERS, CHOPPED FINELY
- 2 TABLESPOONS FRESH DILL SPRIGS, EXTRA

1 Preheat oven to 240°C/475°F.

2 Wash unpeeled potatoes; cut into wedges. Combine potato, unpeeled garlic and 1 tablespoon of the oil in a large baking dish; season. Roast, uncovered, for 20 minutes.

3 Meanwhile, fill fish cavities with lemon and ¼ cup of the dill; season. Place fish on top of potato; drizzle with remaining oil. Roast, uncovered, for 25 minutes or until fish and potato are cooked through.

4 Finely chop remaining dill. Combine mayonnaise, horseradish cream, capers and chopped dill in a small bowl.

5 Serve fish and potatoes topped with extra dill, and with the horseradish mayonnaise.

tips The recipe can be doubled to serve 4; use two baking dishes for even cooking.

Recipe is not suitable to freeze.

serving suggestion Serve with a green salad.

CREAMY PRAWN & FISH PIE

PREP + COOK TIME **1½ HOURS** SERVES **8**

- 1 LITRE (4 CUPS) MILK
- 1 MEDIUM LEEK (350G), SLICED THINLY
- 1 TRIMMED CELERY STICK (100G), SLICED THINLY
- 400G (12½ OUNCES) SKINLESS FIRM WHITE FISH FILLETS, CUT INTO 3CM (1¼-INCH) PIECES
- 400G (12½ OUNCES) SKINLESS SALMON FILLETS, CUT INTO 3CM (1¼-INCH) PIECES
- 80G (2½ OUNCES) BUTTER
- ½ CUP (75G) PLAIN (ALL-PURPOSE) FLOUR
- 1 CUP (120G) GRATED CHEDDAR
- 400G (12½ OUNCES) UNCOOKED PEELED MEDIUM KING PRAWNS (SHRIMP)
- 400G (12½ OUNCES) SMOKED FISH (SUCH AS TROUT, HADDOCK OR COD), SKIN REMOVED, FLAKED
- 2 TABLESPOONS FINELY CHOPPED FRESH DILL
- 2 TEASPOONS FINELY GRATED LEMON RIND
- 1 TABLESPOON LEMON JUICE
- 30G (1 OUNCE) BUTTER, CHOPPED FINELY, EXTRA
- 2 SPRIGS FRESH DILL, EXTRA

MASH

- 1.2KG (2½ POUNDS) DESIREE POTATOES
- ⅓ CUP (80ML) MILK, WARMED
- 90G (3 OUNCES) BUTTER, CHOPPED

1 Place milk, leek and celery in a large saucepan over medium heat; bring to a simmer. Add fish; simmer, uncovered, over low heat, for 10 minutes or until fish is cooked through. Strain milk mixture over a large bowl. Transfer fish and vegetables to a medium bowl.
2 Meanwhile, make mash.
3 Preheat oven to 180°C/350°F.
4 Heat butter in cleaned saucepan over medium-high heat, add flour; cook, stirring, until mixture thickens and bubbles. Gradually add reserved milk; whisk until mixture boils and thickens. Add cheese; stir until smooth. Add cooked fish, prawns, smoked fish, dill, rind and juice; stir to combine. Season. Remove from heat.
5 Transfer fish mixture to a 3-litre (12-cup) ovenproof dish; top evenly with mash. Using a fork, swirl mash in a decorative pattern; dot with extra butter.
6 Bake pie for 45 minutes or until heated through and mash is golden. Serve topped with extra dill.
mash Boil, steam or microwave potato until tender; drain. Mash potato with warmed milk and butter in a large bowl until smooth; season to taste.

tips We used flathead for the firm white fish fillets.

Pie can be made to the end of step 4 up to 6 hours ahead.

Recipe is not suitable to freeze.

EGGPLANT PARMIGIANA

PREP + COOK TIME **1¼ HOURS** SERVES **4**

⅔ CUP (160ML) OLIVE OIL

1 MEDIUM BROWN ONION
   (150G), CHOPPED FINELY

2 CLOVES GARLIC, CRUSHED

400G (12½ OUNCES) CANNED
   DICED TOMATOES

2 CUPS (560G) BOTTLED
   TOMATO PASSATA

¼ TEASPOON DRIED
   CHILLI FLAKES

2 MEDIUM EGGPLANTS (600G),
   SLICED THICKLY

¼ CUP (35G) PLAIN
   (ALL-PURPOSE) FLOUR

⅓ CUP LOOSELY PACKED
   FRESH BASIL LEAVES,
   PLUS EXTRA TO SERVE

200G (6½ OUNCES)
   BOCCONCINI,
   SLICED THINLY

⅔ CUP (50G) FINELY
   GRATED PARMESAN

½ TEASPOON SWEET PAPRIKA

1 Preheat oven to 180°C/350°F.

2 Heat 1 tablespoon of the oil in a large frying pan over medium heat; cook onion, stirring, until soft. Add garlic; cook, stirring, until fragrant. Stir in tomatoes, passata and chilli; season to taste. Transfer mixture to a medium jug.

3 Toss eggplant in flour to coat; shake off excess. Heat remaining oil in same pan; cook eggplant, in batches, until browned on both sides. Drain on paper towel.

4 Layer half the eggplant in a 18cm x 25cm (7¼-inch x 10-inch) ovenproof dish; season. Top with half the tomato mixture, basil and bocconcini. Repeat layering, finishing with parmesan. Sprinkle with paprika.

5 Bake, covered, for 30 minutes. Uncover, bake for a further 15 minutes or until browned and tender. Serve topped with extra basil.

tip *Recipe is not suitable to freeze.*

serving suggestions *Serve with a rocket (arugula) salad and crusty bread or stir through cooked short pasta.*

ZUCCHINI, BLACK BEAN & CORN ENCHILADAS

PREP + COOK TIME **1¾ HOURS** SERVES **4**

3 LARGE ZUCCHINI (450G)

⅓ CUP (80ML) OLIVE OIL

2 TRIMMED CORN COBS (500G)

8 X 20CM (8-INCH) WHITE CORN TORTILLAS

400G (12½ OUNCES) CANNED BLACK BEANS, DRAINED, RINSED

½ CUP LOOSELY PACKED FRESH CORIANDER (CILANTRO) LEAVES

100G (3 OUNCES) FETTA

¼ CUP LOOSELY PACKED FRESH OREGANO LEAVES

1 TABLESPOON FRESH OREGANO, EXTRA

ENCHILADA SAUCE

800G (1½ POUNDS) CANNED CRUSHED TOMATOES

1½ CUPS (375ML) VEGETABLE STOCK

2 TABLESPOONS OLIVE OIL

2 TABLESPOONS COARSELY CHOPPED FRESH OREGANO

2 TABLESPOONS APPLE CIDER VINEGAR

1 MEDIUM BROWN ONION (150G), CHOPPED COARSELY

1 CLOVE GARLIC, CHOPPED

1 TABLESPOON CHOPPED PICKLED JALAPEÑOS

1 TEASPOON GROUND CUMIN

1 TEASPOON CASTER (SUPERFINE) SUGAR

¼ TEASPOON CHILLI POWDER

1 Preheat oven to 180°C/350°F. Line an oven tray with baking paper. Grease a 25cm x 30cm (10-inch x 12-inch) ovenproof dish.

2 Cut zucchini in half lengthways then cut each half into long thin wedges. Place zucchini on tray; drizzle with half the oil. Roast for 30 minutes or until just tender; chop coarsely.

3 Meanwhile, make enchilada sauce.

4 Brush corn with 1 tablespoon of the oil. Heat a grill plate (or grill or barbecue) to medium-high heat; cook corn, turning occasionally, for 10 minutes or until golden and tender. Cut kernels from cobs; discard cobs.

5 Reheat grill plate to medium-high heat; cook tortillas, for 30 seconds each side or until lightly charred. Transfer to a plate; cover to keep warm.

6 Combine zucchini, beans, coriander, half the corn, half the fetta, half the oregano and ½ cup enchilada sauce in a large bowl.

7 Divide zucchini filling evenly among warm tortillas; roll to enclose filling. Place tortillas in dish; brush tops with remaining oil. Spoon remaining enchilada sauce over tortillas, leaving 2cm (¾-inch) at each end of enchiladas uncovered. Top with remaining fetta and oregano.

8 Bake for 30 minutes or until golden and heated through. Serve topped with remaining corn and extra oregano.

enchilada sauce Blend or process ingredients until smooth; transfer to a medium saucepan. Bring to a simmer over medium heat for 20 minutes or until thickened slightly.

tip Recipe is not suitable to freeze.

SLOW
COOKER

POACHED CHICKEN WITH SOY & SESAME

PREP + COOK TIME **6½ HOURS** SERVES **4**

- **1.6KG (3¼-POUND) WHOLE CHICKEN**
- **5CM (2-INCH) PIECE FRESH GINGER (25G), SLICED THINLY**
- **4 CLOVES GARLIC, HALVED**
- **2 STAR ANISE**
- **2 CINNAMON STICKS**
- **1 CUP (250ML) LIGHT SOY SAUCE**
- **1 CUP (250ML) CHINESE COOKING WINE (SHAO HSING)**
- **⅓ CUP (75G) WHITE (GRANULATED) SUGAR**
- **1 LITRE (4 CUPS) WATER**
- **⅓ CUP (80ML) LIGHT SOY SAUCE, EXTRA**
- **2 TEASPOONS SESAME OIL**
- **2 CLOVES GARLIC, EXTRA, CUT INTO MATCHSTICKS**
- **2.5CM (1-INCH) PIECE FRESH GINGER (15G), EXTRA, CUT INTO MATCHSTICKS**
- **2 FRESH LONG RED CHILLIES, SLICED THINLY**
- **⅓ CUP (80ML) PEANUT OIL**
- **4 GREEN ONIONS (SCALLIONS), SLICED THINLY**
- **½ CUP LOOSELY PACKED FRESH CORIANDER (CILANTRO) LEAVES**

1 Trim excess fat from chicken. Place chicken in a 4.5-litre (18-cup) slow cooker. Add ginger, garlic, star anise, cinnamon, sauce, wine, sugar and the water to cooker. Cook, covered, on low, about 6 hours. Remove chicken from cooker; discard poaching liquid.

2 Cut chicken into 12 pieces; place on a heatproof platter. Drizzle extra sauce and sesame oil over chicken; sprinkle with extra garlic, ginger and chilli.

3 Heat peanut oil in a small saucepan, over medium heat, until very hot; carefully drizzle over chicken. Top with onion and coriander.

tips *Chinese cooking wine is also known as chinese rice wine. Dry sherry can be used instead.*

Recipe is suitable to freeze at the end of step 1 for up to 3 months.

serving suggestion *Serve with steamed noodles or rice.*

BOURBON-GLAZED
BEEF RIBS

PREP + COOK TIME **8½ HOURS** SERVES **4**

- **1 MEDIUM BROWN ONION (150G), CHOPPED FINELY**
- **5 CLOVES GARLIC, CHOPPED COARSELY**
- **½ CUP (140G) TOMATO SAUCE (KETCHUP)**
- **½ CUP (140G) SWEET CHILLI SAUCE**
- **⅓ CUP (80ML) LIGHT SOY SAUCE**
- **½ CUP (125ML) BOURBON**
- **½ CUP (175G) HONEY**
- **8 BEEF SHORT RIBS (2KG)**

1 Combine onion, garlic, sauces, bourbon and honey in a 4.5-litre (18-cup) slow cooker. Add beef; turn to coat in mixture. Cook, covered, on low, about 8 hours. Carefully remove beef from cooker; cover to keep warm.

2 Transfer the sauce to a large frying pan; bring to the boil. Boil, skimming fat from surface, for 10 minutes or until sauce reduces to 2 cups.

3 Spoon sauce over beef to serve.

tips Short ribs are sections of beef ribs usually taken from the second to the tenth rib. Each 'slab' can contain from two to eight ribs. The meat is full of flavour but very tough so it is best braised slowly over low heat.

Recipe is suitable to freeze at the end of step 1.

serving suggestion Serve with thinly sliced fried potatoes.

MASSAMAN BEEF CURRY

PREP + COOK TIME **8¾ HOURS** SERVES **6**

2 TABLESPOONS PEANUT OIL

2 LARGE BROWN ONIONS (400G), CUT INTO THIN WEDGES

1KG (2 POUNDS) GRAVY BEEF, CHOPPED COARSELY

⅔ CUP (200G) MASSAMAN CURRY PASTE

1 CUP (250ML) COCONUT MILK

1 CUP (250ML) CHICKEN STOCK

2 CINNAMON STICKS

2 DRIED BAY LEAVES

3 MEDIUM POTATOES (600G), CHOPPED COARSELY

½ CUP (70G) ROASTED UNSALTED PEANUTS

2 TABLESPOONS LIGHT BROWN SUGAR

1 TABLESPOON FISH SAUCE

⅓ CUP LIGHTLY PACKED FRESH CORIANDER (CILANTRO) LEAVES

1 LIME, CUT INTO WEDGES

1 Heat half the oil in a large frying pan; cook onion, stirring, for 10 minutes or until browned lightly. Transfer to a 4.5-litre (18-cup) slow cooker.

2 Heat remaining oil in same pan; cook beef, in batches, until browned. Add paste; cook, stirring, for 1 minute or until fragrant. Transfer to cooker.

3 Add coconut milk, stock, cinnamon, bay leaves, potato and nuts to cooker. Cook, covered, on low, for about 8 hours.

4 Discard cinnamon sticks. Stir in sugar and sauce. Serve curry sprinkled with coriander; accompany with lime wedges.

tips *Chuck steak is also suitable for this recipe.*

Recipe is not suitable to freeze.

MEXICAN BEEF
CHILLI MOLE

PREP + COOK TIME **8¾ HOURS** SERVES **4**

- 1KG (2 POUNDS) BEEF CHUCK STEAK, CUT INTO 3CM (1¼-INCH) CUBES
- 2 CUPS (500ML) BEEF STOCK
- 2 CUPS (500ML) WATER
- 3 CHIPOTLE PEPPERS IN ADOBO SAUCE, CHOPPED FINELY
- 4 RINDLESS BACON SLICES (260G), CHOPPED COARSELY
- 1 MEDIUM BROWN ONION (150G), CHOPPED FINELY
- 4 CLOVES GARLIC, CRUSHED
- 2 TABLESPOONS TOMATO PASTE
- 439G (14 OUNCES) CANNED BLACK BEANS, DRAINED, RINSED
- 410G (13 OUNCES) CANNED TOMATO PUREE
- 2 TEASPOONS EACH GROUND CUMIN, GROUND CORIANDER AND SWEET SMOKED PAPRIKA
- ¼ TEASPOON CHILLI POWDER
- ½ TEASPOON GROUND CINNAMON
- 2 TABLESPOONS FINELY GRATED MEXICAN CHOCOLATE
- ⅔ CUP (80G) GRATED MANCHEGO CHEESE
- 1 FRESH JALAPEÑO CHILLI, SLICED THINLY
- 2 GREEN ONIONS (SCALLIONS), SLICED THINLY

1 Combine beef, stock, the water, chipotle, bacon, brown onion, garlic, paste, beans, puree and spices in a 4.5-litre (18-cup) slow cooker. Cook, covered, on low, for about 8 hours. Season to taste.

2 Stir chocolate into cooker; season to taste.

3 Serve beef topped with cheese, jalapeño and green onion.

tips Chipotle in adobo sauce and mexican chocolate are available from specialist delicatessens and grocers. If chipotle in adobo sauce is unavailable use 2-3 tablespoons hot Mexican-style chilli sauce (adding enough to suit your taste). If mexican chocolate is unavailable use dark (semi-sweet) chocolate.

Manchego is an aged, hard, intensely flavoured Spanish cheese. It is available from Spanish delicatessens and specialist cheese shops; substitute haloumi or fetta if not available.

If fresh jalapeño chillies are unavailable, use slices of bottled pickled jalapeño.

Suitable to freeze at the end of step 2.

TUSCAN
BEEF STEW

PREP + COOK TIME **6½ HOURS** SERVES **6**

6 PIECES BEEF OSSO BUCO (1.2KG)
1 TABLESPOON OLIVE OIL
1 LARGE BROWN ONION (200G), CHOPPED COARSELY
3 CLOVES GARLIC, CRUSHED
6 ANCHOVY FILLETS, DRAINED, CHOPPED FINELY
2 TABLESPOONS PLAIN (ALL-PURPOSE) FLOUR
¼ CUP (60ML) BALSAMIC VINEGAR
2 TABLESPOONS TOMATO PASTE
400G (12½ OUNCES) CANNED CRUSHED TOMATOES
1 CUP (250ML) BEEF STOCK
¼ CUP (60ML) WATER
4 SPRIGS FRESH ROSEMARY
1 CUP (120G) SEEDED GREEN OLIVES

1 Trim excess fat from beef. Heat oil in a large frying pan over medium-high heat. Cook beef, in batches, until browned. Transfer to a 4.5-litre (18-cup) slow cooker.
2 Add onion, garlic and anchovy to same pan; cook, stirring, for 1 minute or until fragrant. Add flour; cook, stirring, about 1 minute. Stir in vinegar and paste, then tomatoes, stock, the water and rosemary. Transfer mixture to cooker.
3 Cook, covered, on low, for about 6 hours. Season to taste.
4 Just before serving, stir in olives.

tips In Italian, osso buco literally means 'bone with a hole'. It is cut from the shin of the hind leg (shank) and is also known as knuckle. The hole is filled with rich bone marrow, also known as 'jelly'; stand the bones upright to cook, so you don't lose the delicious jelly inside.

Recipe is suitable to freeze at the end of step 3.

serving suggestion Serve with soft polenta and baby rocket (arugula) leaves.

PEPPERED
PORK CURRY

PREP + COOK TIME **8½ HOURS** SERVES **4**

- **1.2KG (2½ POUNDS) DICED BONELESS PORK SHOULDER**
- **1 MEDIUM RED ONION (170G), SLICED THINLY**
- **4 CLOVES GARLIC, CRUSHED**
- **4 TEASPOONS FINELY GRATED FRESH GINGER**
- **2 TABLESPOONS BROWN SUGAR**
- **2 TEASPOONS CRACKED BLACK PEPPER**
- **1 CINNAMON STICK**
- **2 TEASPOONS GROUND CUMIN**
- **1 TEASPOON GROUND FENUGREEK**
- **½ TEASPOON GROUND CARDAMOM**
- **1 CUP (250ML) CHICKEN STOCK**
- **400G (12½ OUNCES) CANNED DICED TOMATOES**
- **1 CUP (280G) GREEK-STYLE YOGHURT**
- **150G (4½ OUNCES) BABY SPINACH LEAVES**
- **⅓ CUP LOOSELY PACKED FRESH CORIANDER (CILANTRO) LEAVES**

1 Combine pork, onion, garlic, ginger, sugar, spices, stock, tomatoes and half the yoghurt in a 5-litre (20-cup) slow cooker. Cook, covered, on low, for about 8 hours.

2 Discard cinnamon. Add spinach and remaining yoghurt to cooker; cook, uncovered, on high, for 5 minutes or until spinach wilts. Season to taste.

3 Serve the curry sprinkled with coriander; top with extra yoghurt, if you like.

tip Recipe is suitable to freeze at the end of step 1.

serving suggestion Serve with steamed rice and warmed roti bread.

LAMB SHANK & SPINACH KORMA CURRY

PREP + COOK TIME **8½ HOURS** SERVES **6**

6 FRENCH-TRIMMED LAMB SHANKS (1.5KG)
400G (12½ OUNCES) CANNED CRUSHED TOMATOES
1 LARGE BROWN ONION (200G), SLICED THICKLY
300ML POURING CREAM
100G (3 OUNCES) BABY SPINACH LEAVES
1 CUP (120G) FROZEN PEAS

KORMA PASTE

1 TABLESPOON CUMIN SEEDS
3 CLOVES GARLIC, QUARTERED
5CM (2-INCH) PIECE FRESH GINGER (25G), GRATED FINELY
⅓ CUP (50G) TOASTED CASHEW NUTS
¼ CUP (60ML) TOMATO SAUCE (KETCHUP)
¼ CUP COARSELY CHOPPED CORIANDER (CILANTRO) ROOT AND STEM MIXTURE
2 TABLESPOONS DESICCATED COCONUT
1 TABLESPOON GARAM MASALA
2 TEASPOONS EACH GROUND CORIANDER, GROUND TURMERIC AND SEA SALT FLAKES
¼ CUP (60ML) VEGETABLE OIL

1 Make korma paste.
2 Combine lamb, tomatoes, onion, cream and paste in a 4.5-litre (18-cup) slow cooker. Cook, covered, on low, for about 8 hours.
3 Add spinach and peas to cooker; cook, covered, for 10 minutes or until heated through.

korma paste Place cumin in a small frying pan; cook, stirring, for 1 minute or until fragrant. Remove from heat. Blend or process cumin with remaining ingredients until smooth.

tips Suitable to freeze at the end of step 2. Korma paste can be frozen separately.

serving suggestion Serve with steamed basmati rice, yoghurt and naan bread.

SMOKY STICKY PORK RIBS WITH COLESLAW

PREP + COOK TIME **4¾ HOURS** SERVES **4**

2KG (4 POUNDS) AMERICAN-STYLE PORK RIBS
3 CLOVES GARLIC, CRUSHED
1 CUP (280G) BARBECUE SAUCE
¼ CUP (60ML) LEMON JUICE
¼ CUP (55G) BROWN SUGAR
2 TEASPOONS SWEET SMOKED PAPRIKA
1 TEASPOON TABASCO SAUCE

COLESLAW
¼ SMALL GREEN CABBAGE (300G), SHREDDED FINELY
¼ SMALL RED CABBAGE (300G), SHREDDED FINELY
1 LARGE CARROT (180G), GRATED COARSELY
½ SMALL RED ONION (50G), SLICED THINLY
1 CUP (120G) COARSELY GRATED VINTAGE CHEDDAR
2 TABLESPOONS COARSELY CHOPPED FRESH CHIVES
¾ CUP (225G) MAYONNAISE
¼ CUP (60ML) APPLE CIDER VINEGAR

1 Cut pork into pieces that will fit into a 4.5-litre (18-cup) slow cooker.
2 Combine remaining ingredients in a large shallow dish; add pork, turn to coat in marinade. Transfer pork and marinade to cooker. Cook, covered, on high, for about 4 hours. Turn ribs twice during cooking time for even cooking.
3 Make coleslaw.
4 Carefully remove ribs from cooker; cover to keep warm. Transfer sauce to a medium frying pan; bring to the boil. Reduce heat; simmer, uncovered, skimming fat from surface, for 10 minutes or until sauce has reduced to 1 cup.
5 Drizzle pork with sauce. Serve with coleslaw.
coleslaw Combine ingredients in a large bowl; toss gently to combine. Season to taste.

tips Ask the butcher to cut the ribs into pieces that will fit into your slow cooker.

Recipe is not suitable to freeze.

SPLIT PEA & CAPSICUM CURRY

PREP + COOK TIME **8½ HOURS** SERVES **4**

- **1 MEDIUM BROWN ONION (150G), SLICED THINLY**
- **500G (1 POUND) BABY NEW POTATOES, HALVED**
- **1 LARGE CARROT (180G), HALVED, SLICED THICKLY**
- **1 MEDIUM RED CAPSICUM (BELL PEPPER) (350G), CHOPPED COARSELY**
- **1 MEDIUM YELLOW CAPSICUM (BELL PEPPER) (350G), CHOPPED COARSELY**
- **⅓ CUP (100G) MILD INDIAN CURRY PASTE**
- **⅓ CUP (85G) YELLOW SPLIT PEAS**
- **⅓ CUP (85G) GREEN SPLIT PEAS**
- **8 FRESH CURRY LEAVES**
- **2 TABLESPOONS TOMATO PASTE**
- **410G (13 OUNCES) CANNED CRUSHED TOMATOES**
- **2 CUPS (500ML) VEGETABLE STOCK**
- **2 CUPS (500ML) WATER**
- **150G (4½ OUNCES) SUGAR SNAP PEAS**
- **1 BUNCH CAVOLO NERO (TUSCAN CABBAGE) (400G), CHOPPED COARSELY**
- **¾ CUP (200G) GREEK-STYLE YOGHURT**
- **½ CUP LOOSELY PACKED FRESH CORIANDER (CILANTRO) LEAVES**

1 Place onion, potato, carrot, capsicums, curry paste, split peas, curry leaves, tomato paste, tomatoes, stock and the water in a 4.5-litre (18-cup) slow cooker. Cook, covered, on low, for about 8 hours. Season to taste.

2 Stir in sugar snap peas and cavolo nero. Cook, uncovered, on low, for 10 minutes or until peas and cavolo nero are tender.

3 Serve curry topped with yoghurt and sprinkled with coriander.

tip Recipe is not suitable to freeze.

serving suggestion Serve with steamed rice and pappadums.

VEGETABLE STEW
WITH POLENTA DUMPLINGS

PREP + COOK TIME **9 HOURS** SERVES **4**

- **1 MEDIUM RED ONION (170G), CUT INTO WEDGES**
- **2 MEDIUM ZUCCHINI (240G), SLICED THICKLY**
- **4 YELLOW PATTY PAN SQUASH (120G), CUT INTO WEDGES**
- **1 MEDIUM KUMARA (ORANGE SWEET POTATO) (400G), CHOPPED COARSELY**
- **2 MEDIUM CARROTS (240G), CHOPPED COARSELY**
- **1 TRIMMED CORN COB (250G), CUT INTO 6 ROUNDS**
- **1 MEDIUM RED CAPSICUM (BELL PEPPER) (350G), CHOPPED COARSELY**
- **2 FLAT MUSHROOMS (160G) CUT INTO WEDGES**
- **3 CLOVES GARLIC, CRUSHED**
- **30G (1-OUNCE) SACHET TACO SEASONING**
- **2 TEASPOONS PAPRIKA**
- **800G (1½ POUNDS) CANNED CRUSHED TOMATOES**
- **1 CUP (250ML) VEGETABLE STOCK**
- **2 TABLESPOONS FRESH FLAT-LEAF PARSLEY LEAVES**

POLENTA DUMPLINGS
- **1 CUP (150G) SELF-RAISING FLOUR**
- **2 TABLESPOONS POLENTA (CORNMEAL)**
- **60G (2 OUNCES) COLD BUTTER, CHOPPED**
- **1 EGG, BEATEN LIGHTLY**
- **¼ CUP (20G) FINELY GRATED PARMESAN**
- **2 TABLESPOONS MILK, APPROXIMATELY**

1 Place onion, zucchini, squash, kumara, carrot, corn, capsicum, mushroom, garlic, seasoning, paprika, tomatoes and stock in a 4.5-litre (18-cup) slow cooker. Cook, covered, on low, for about 8 hours.
2 Make polenta dumpling mixture just before required.
3 Drop level tablespoons of dumpling mixture, about 2cm (¾ inch) apart, on top of stew. Cook, covered, on low, for 30 minutes or until dumplings are firm to touch and cooked through. Serve stew and dumplings with parsley.

polenta dumplings Place flour and polenta in a medium bowl; rub in butter. Stir in egg, parmesan and enough milk to make a soft, sticky dough.

tips Add drained, rinsed canned kidney beans or trimmed green beans for the last 10 minutes of cooking time.

Recipe is not suitable to freeze.

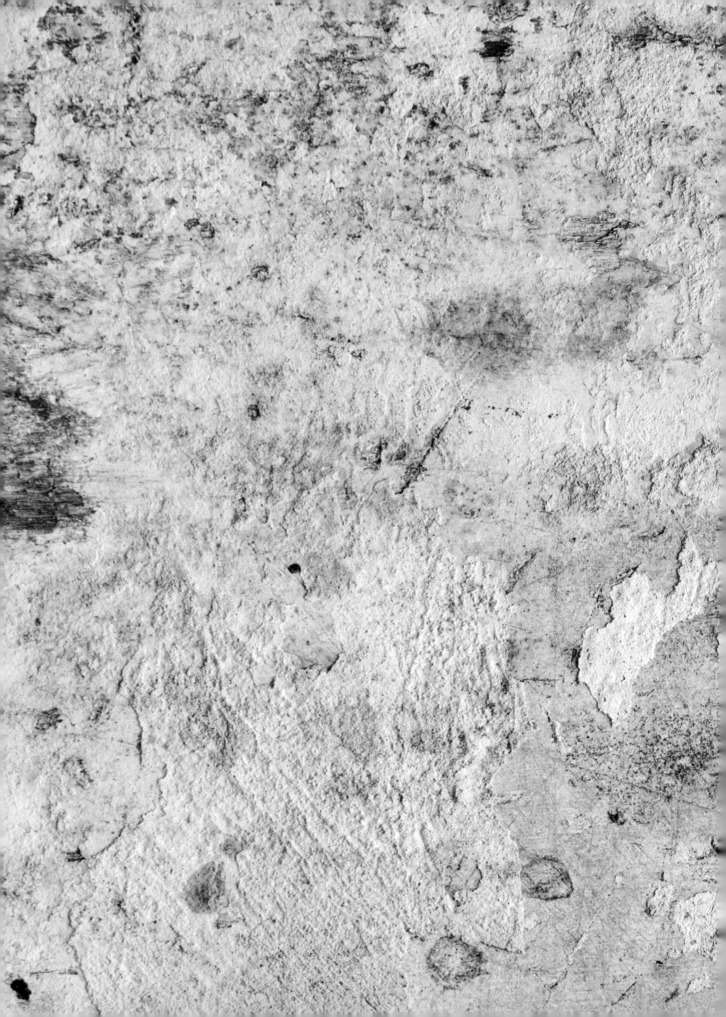

BREADS

DARK SPICED RYE BREAD

PREP + COOK TIME **3¾ HOURS (+ STANDING)** MAKES **3 LOAVES**

- 4 TEASPOONS (14G) DRIED YEAST
- 2 TEASPOONS CASTER (SUPERFINE) SUGAR
- 2 CUPS (500ML) WARM WATER
- ½ CUP (125ML) EXTRA VIRGIN OLIVE OIL
- ¼ CUP (95G) MOLASSES
- 1 TABLESPOON CARAWAY SEEDS
- 1 TEASPOON CUMIN SEEDS, TOASTED
- ½ CUP (75G) SUNFLOWER SEED KERNELS
- 2 LARGE CARROTS (360G), PEELED, GRATED COARSELY
- 1 CUP (170G) FINE CORNMEAL (MAIZE FLOUR)
- 3 CUPS (450G) RYE FLOUR
- 1 CUP (300G) PLAIN (ALL-PURPOSE) FLOUR
- ⅓ CUP (35G) DUTCH-PROCESSED COCOA
- 1 TABLESPOON FINE SALT
- ½ CUP (75G) PLAIN (ALL-PURPOSE) FLOUR, EXTRA

1 Whisk yeast, sugar and the water in a large bowl until yeast is dissolved. Cover; stand in a warm place for 10 minutes or until mixture is frothy.

2 Stir oil and molasses into yeast mixture, then seeds, carrot, cornmeal and sifted flours, cocoa and salt to form a slightly sticky dough. Turn dough onto a well-floured surface; knead for 10 minutes or until smooth, dusting the surface frequently with the extra flour. Place dough in a large oiled bowl. Cover; stand in a warm place for 1¾ hours or until dough has doubled in size.

3 Turn dough onto a floured surface; divide into three portions. Knead each portion until smooth. Shape each portion into a 12cm (4¾-inch) round. Place on two baking-paper-lined oven trays (place two on one tray and one on the second tray); cover with clean tea towels, stand in a warm place for 45 minutes or until dough has risen slightly.

4 Preheat oven to 200°C/400°F.

5 Dust loaves with a little more plain flour, then using a small, floured sharp knife, make five or six slashes, in both directions, across each loaf.

6 Bake bread for 40 minutes (swapping trays between shelves halfway through cooking time) or until hollow sounding when tapped. (It is not necessary to swap the trays around in a fan-forced oven as the fan will circulate the heat more evenly.) Transfer loaves to wire racks to cool. Leave for at least 45 minutes before eating.

tip Bread will keep for up to 3 days.

serving suggestion Serve with smoked salmon or as a breakfast or sandwich bread.

BUTTERY FRENCH
BRIOCHE

PREP + COOK TIME **1 HOUR (+ STANDING & REFRIGERATION)**
MAKES **1 LOAF**

You will need to start this recipe the day before.

4 TEASPOONS (14G) DRY YEAST
⅓ CUP (80ML) WARM WATER
¼ CUP (55G) CASTER (SUPERFINE) SUGAR
4 CUPS (600G) PLAIN (ALL-PURPOSE) FLOUR
1 TEASPOON FINE SALT
5 EGGS, BEATEN LIGHTLY
250G (8 OUNCES) BUTTER
1 EGG, EXTRA, BEATEN LIGHTLY
1 TABLESPOON CASTER (SUPERFINE) SUGAR, EXTRA

1 Whisk yeast, the water and 1 tablespoon of the caster sugar in a small bowl until yeast dissolves. Cover; stand in a warm place for 10 minutes or until mixture is frothy.
2 Sift flour, salt and remaining caster sugar into a large bowl, then add yeast mixture and egg; stir until just combined. Turn dough onto a floured surface, knead for 10 minutes or until dough is smooth and elastic.
3 Divide butter into 10 equal portions. Knead each portion of butter into dough, kneading well after each addition, until all the butter is incorporated and dough is smooth and glossy. Place dough into a large bowl; cover, refrigerate overnight.
4 Preheat oven to 200°C/400°F.
5 Divide dough into three equal portions; roll each portion into a 45cm (18-inch) length. Place dough lengths on a large greased oven tray; cross lengths over and under each other into a plait. Cover; stand in a cool place for 1 hour or until dough has nearly doubled in size.

6 Brush plait with extra egg; sprinkle with extra sugar. Bake brioche for 10 minutes. Reduce heat to 180°C/350°F; bake for a further 20 minutes or until golden and bread sounds hollow when tapped.

tips *While this bread can be kneaded by hand, it is much easier to incorporate the butter using a bench mixer and dough hook.*

Brioche will keep for up to 2 days. Freeze for up to 3 months.

serving suggestion *Serve with soft scrambled eggs and smoked salmon, or with any jams or marmalades.*

SEEDED PUMPKIN
BREAD STICKS

PREP + COOK TIME **2 HOURS (+ STANDING)** MAKES **6 STICKS**

900G (1¾-POUND) BUTTERNUT PUMPKIN, HALVED LENGTHWAYS, SEEDS REMOVED

2 TEASPOONS (7G) DRIED YEAST

1 TABLESPOON HONEY

½ CUP (125ML) LUKEWARM WATER

2 TABLESPOONS VEGETABLE OIL

1⅓ CUPS (200G) WHOLEMEAL PLAIN (ALL-PURPOSE) FLOUR

2 CUPS (300G) '00' FLOUR, BREAD FLOUR OR PLAIN (ALL-PURPOSE) FLOUR

½ CUP (75G) SUNFLOWER SEEDS

2 TABLESPOONS SESAME SEEDS

1 TABLESPOON LINSEEDS (FLAXSEEDS)

1 TABLESPOON SEA SALT FLAKES

1 EGG, BEATEN LIGHTLY

¼ CUP PEPITAS (PUMPKIN SEED KERNELS)

1 TABLESPOON POPPY SEEDS

2 TABLESPOONS SUNFLOWER SEED KERNELS, EXTRA

1 Preheat oven to 180°C/350°F.

2 Place pumpkin on an oven tray, cover with foil; bake for 1¼ hours or until very tender. When cool enough to handle, scoop flesh into a medium bowl; mash with a fork. You need 1½ cups mashed pumpkin.

3 Combine yeast, honey and the water in a small bowl; cover with plastic wrap. Stand in a warm place for 10 minutes or until frothy. Stir in oil.

4 Combine sifted flours, sunflower, sesame and linseed seeds, and salt in a large bowl. Add yeast mixture and mashed pumpkin; mix to a soft dough. Knead dough on a floured surface for 10 minutes or until smooth and elastic. (If you have an electric mixer with a dough hook, mix on medium speed for 6 minutes or until smooth and elastic.)

5 Place dough in a large oiled bowl; cover with plastic wrap. Stand in a warm place for 1 hour or until doubled in size.

6 Increase oven to 200°C/400°F. Punch down dough with your fist.

Knead on a floured surface for 1 minute or until smooth. Roll dough into six 4cm x 30cm (1½-inch x 12-inch) lengths; place on a large oiled oven tray. (Or divide dough into 12 even-sized balls, roll in seeds; see tips.)

7 Cover dough loosely with oiled plastic wrap. Stand in a warm place for 40 minutes or until dough is almost doubled in size.

8 Brush dough with egg, sprinkle with pepitas, poppy seeds and extra sunflower seeds. Bake for 25 minutes or until golden and bread sounds hollow when tapped. Cool on a wire rack.

tips If you'd prefer to make rolls, divide the dough into 12 smooth rounds. Place pepitas and poppy seeds in a small bowl; roll dough rounds in the seeds to coat. Place 1cm (½ inch) apart on an oiled oven tray in a rectangle shape (three across and four down). Continue recipe from step 7.

Bread sticks will keep for up to 3 days.

ROSEMARY KALAMATA OLIVE BREAD

PREP + COOK TIME **1¼ HOURS (+ STANDING)** MAKES **1 LOAF**

2 TEASPOONS (7G) DRIED YEAST

1 TEASPOON CASTER (SUPERFINE) SUGAR

1¼ CUPS (310ML) WARM MILK

3⅓ CUPS (500G) PLAIN (ALL-PURPOSE) FLOUR

1 TEASPOON SALT

¼ CUP (60ML) EXTRA VIRGIN OLIVE OIL

1 CUP (120G) PITTED KALAMATA OLIVES, CHOPPED FINELY

1 TABLESPOON FRESH CHOPPED ROSEMARY

1 Combine yeast, sugar and milk in a small jug; stand in a warm place for 15 minutes or until mixture is frothy.

2 Sift flour and salt into a large bowl. Stir in yeast mixture and oil; mix to a firm dough. Knead dough on a floured surface for 5 minutes or until smooth and elastic. Place dough in an oiled bowl; cover, stand in a warm place for 1 hour 20 minutes or until dough has doubled in size.

3 Turn dough onto a lightly floured surface; knead until smooth. Press the dough into a 23cm x 28cm (9¼-inch x 11¼-inch) rectangle. Spread olives and rosemary over dough, leaving a 2cm (¾-inch) border. Roll up dough from the long side, tuck ends underneath; place on a lightly greased oven tray.

4 Sift a little extra flour over bread. Holding scissors vertically, make cuts about 2.5cm (1-inch) apart, along centre of bread. Place bread in a warm place; stand, uncovered, for 1½ hours or until doubled in size.

5 Meanwhile, preheat oven to 180°C/350°F.

6 Bake for 45 minutes or until bread is browned and sounds hollow when tapped.

tip This recipe is best made on the day of serving.

serving suggestion Serve toasted with soup, or topped with vine-ripened tomatoes and torn mozzarella drizzled with olive oil.

NO-KNEAD SPELT
LINSEED & CUMIN
BREAD

PREP + COOK TIME **45 MINUTES (+ STANDING)** MAKES **1 LOAF**

2 TEASPOONS (7G) DRIED YEAST
1⅓ CUPS (330ML) LUKEWARM WATER
1⅓ CUPS (200G) ORGANIC WHOLEMEAL SPELT FLOUR
⅓ CUP (60G) LINSEEDS (FLAXSEEDS)
2 TEASPOONS CUMIN SEEDS
1 TABLESPOON OLIVE OIL
2 TEASPOONS GOLDEN SYRUP
2 TEASPOONS SEA SALT
2 CUPS (300G) BREAD FLOUR
1 TEASPOON BREAD FLOUR, EXTRA
1 TEASPOON CUMIN SEEDS, EXTRA

1 Place yeast and the water in a large bowl; whisk until combined. Add spelt flour, seeds, oil and syrup; stir until combined.

2 Add salt and bread flour; mix into a sticky dough. Cover bowl with plastic wrap; stand in a warm place for 1 hour or until dough has doubled in size.

3 Turn dough out onto a lightly floured work surface; press out to form a 25cm (10-inch) round. Fold the dough under itself to form a 16cm (6½-inch) round loaf. Place seam-side down on a baking-paper-lined oven tray. Dust with extra flour; cover with a clean tea towel. Stand in a warm place for 45 minutes or until almost doubled in size.

4 Preheat oven to 220°C/425°F.

5 Using a small sharp knife, score five straight lines across the top of the bread. Sprinkle with extra cumin seeds. Bake for 30 minutes or until bread is browned and sounds hollow when tapped.

tip Bread will keep for up to 4 days.

serving suggestion
Serve with savoury dishes or in sandwiches.

BASIC PIDE &
FOUR TOPPINGS
(See recipes pages 174 & 175)

photograph page 173

BASIC PIDE &
FOUR TOPPINGS

Make our basic pide dough and then choose which topping you would like on it.
Each pide recipe serves 6. For a pide party, quadruple the dough and make all four toppings.

BASIC PIDE DOUGH

PREP TIME **30 MINUTES (+ STANDING)**

1 TEASPOON (4G) DRIED YEAST
1 TEASPOON CASTER
(SUPERFINE) SUGAR
2 TABLESPOONS WARM MILK
⅔ CUP (180ML) WARM WATER
2 CUPS (300G) PLAIN
(ALL-PURPOSE) FLOUR
1 TEASPOON SALT
1 TABLESPOON OLIVE OIL

1 Combine yeast, sugar, milk and the water in a jug; stand in a warm place until mixture is frothy.
2 Place ½ cup flour in a bowl; whisk in yeast mixture. Cover; stand in a warm place for 1 hour or until the mixture becomes a little more frothy.
3 Stir remaining flour and salt into yeast mixture with oil. Knead dough on a floured surface until smooth. Place in an oiled bowl, cover; stand in a warm place for 1 hour.
4 Divide dough into 3 pieces; roll each piece into a 12cm x 30cm (4¾-inch x 12-inch) rectangle. Choose a topping; cook as directed.

EGG & CHEESE

PREP + COOK TIME
25 MINUTES

3 EGGS
90G (3 OUNCES) HALOUMI,
GRATED COARSELY
1 GREEN ONION (SCALLIONS),
CHOPPED COARSELY

1 Preheat oven to 240°C/475°F. Heat oven trays in oven for 3 minutes. Place pide dough pieces on hot trays; bake for 5 minutes. Remove from oven and press centre of pide down to flatten.
2 Whisk eggs, cheese and onion in a large jug. Pour into depression in pide. Bake 10 minutes or until set. Serve with lemon wedges and extra green onion.

photograph page 173

LAMB & TOMATO

PREP + COOK TIME
35 MINUTES

1 TABLESPOON OLIVE OIL
**1 MEDIUM ONION (150G),
    CHOPPED FINELY**
1 CLOVE GARLIC, CRUSHED
**300G (9½ OUNCES) MINCED
    (GROUND) LAMB**
**1 TEASPOON GROUND
    CINNAMON**
1 TEASPOON GROUND CUMIN
1 TEASPOON SMOKED PAPRIKA
**½ TEASPOON CAYENNE
    PEPPER**
**1 TABLESPOON CHOPPED
    FRESH CORIANDER
    (CILANTRO)**
**250G (8 OUNCES)
    CHERRY TOMATOES,
    CUT INTO THIN WEDGES**

1 Preheat oven to 240°C/475°F.
2 Heat oil in a pan; cook onion
and garlic. Add lamb and spices;
cook, stirring, until meat is
browned. Stir in coriander; cool.
3 Spread filling across centre of
each piece of pide dough, leaving
a 2cm (¾-inch) border.
4 Heat oven trays for 3 minutes,
place pide on trays; bake for
10 minutes. Top with tomato.
Serve topped with extra coriander
sprigs, if you like.

SPINACH & FETTA

PREP + COOK TIME
25 MINUTES

300G (9½ OUNCES) SPINACH
**100G (3 OUNCES) FETTA,
    CRUMBLED**
**90G (3 OUNCES) HALOUMI,
    GRATED COARSELY**

1 Preheat oven to 240°C/475°F.
2 Boil, steam or microwave
spinach until wilted. Cool under
cold running water, drain then
squeeze out excess water; shred
spinach finely.
3 Combine spinach and cheeses
in a medium bowl. Spread filling
across centre of each piece of
pide dough, leaving a 2cm
(¾-inch) border.
4 Heat oven trays for 3 minutes,
place pide on trays; bake for
15 minutes.

PUMPKIN & FETTA

PREP + COOK TIME
30 MINUTES

**200G (6½ OUNCES) CHOPPED
    PUMPKIN**
**100G (3 OUNCES) FETTA,
    CHOPPED**
**½ CUP (50G) COARSELY
    GRATED MOZZARELLA**
**1 TABLESPOON CHOPPED
    FRESH FLAT-LEAF PARSLEY**

1 Preheat oven to 240°C/475°F.
2 Boil, steam or microwave
pumpkin until tender; drain, cool.
3 Combine pumpkin and
cheeses in a bowl. Spread filling
across centre of each piece of
pide dough, leaving a 2cm
(¾-inch) border.
4 Heat oven trays for 3 minutes,
place pide on trays; bake for
15 minutes. Serve topped with
parsley.

FLATBREAD
ROTI CHANAI

PREP + COOK TIME **1 HOUR (+ STANDING)** MAKES **8**

You will need to start this recipe the day before.

500G (3⅓ CUPS) PLAIN (ALL-PURPOSE) FLOUR
1½ TEASPOONS FINE SEA SALT FLAKES
1 TEASPOON CASTER (SUPERFINE) SUGAR
¾ CUP (180G) GHEE, MELTED
1 EGG
⅔ CUP (160ML) MILK
⅓ CUP (80ML) WATER
2 TABLESPOONS VEGETABLE OIL
2 TABLESPOONS VEGETABLE OIL, EXTRA

1 Combine flour, salt, sugar and 2 tablespoons of the ghee in a large bowl. Using fingertips, rub in ghee until mixture resembles breadcrumbs. Transfer to the bowl of an electric mixer fitted with a dough hook (see tips). Add egg, milk and the water; knead for 12 minutes or until smooth.

2 Place dough in a large well-oiled bowl; turn to coat dough in oil. Cover with plastic wrap; stand dough at room temperature for 20 minutes.

3 Divide dough into eight balls. Add oil to bowl; place balls in bowl, turn to coat in oil; transfer to a baking-paper-lined oven tray. Cover with plastic wrap; stand at room temperature for 5 hours or overnight. (This will relax the gluten developed during kneading, thus producing a tender textured dough.)

4 Working with one ball of dough, and using 1 teaspoon extra oil and the heel of your hand, press dough out on a lightly oiled surface, into a 20cm (8-inch) round. Using oiled hands, carefully stretch the dough out from the centre in a circular motion, pulling it gently until very thin and approximately 50cm (20-inch) round. (Don't worry if a few tears form as you stretch the dough, this doesn't matter and won't be obvious at the end.)

5 Using a pastry brush, dab a little melted ghee over the dough. Fold two sides into the centre to meet; repeat with remaining two sides to form a 15cm (6-inch) square. (Do not press down on the dough.) Transfer to a baking-paper-lined oven tray. Repeat with remaining dough.

6 Heat 1 teaspoon of the ghee in a large frying pan over medium-low heat. Cook roti for 2½ minutes each side or until golden and cooked through. Cover to keep warm. Repeat with remaining ghee and roti.

tip If your electric mixer doesn't have a dough hook attachment, mix the dough using the paddle attachment instead.

CITRUS HAZELNUT
BREAD TWIST

PREP + COOK TIME **1¼ HOURS (+ STANDING)** SERVES **8**

- **3 TEASPOONS (10G) DRIED YEAST**
- **1½ TABLESPOONS CASTER (SUPERFINE) SUGAR**
- **½ CUP (125ML) MILK, WARMED**
- **2 EGG YOLKS**
- **100G (3 OUNCES) BUTTER, MELTED**
- **¾ CUP (180ML) WARM WATER**
- **3 CUPS (450G) PLAIN (ALL-PURPOSE) FLOUR**
- **½ TEASPOON SALT**
- **1 CUP (140G) ROASTED PEELED HAZELNUTS**
- **⅓ CUP (75G) DEMERARA SUGAR**
- **1 TEASPOON MIXED SPICE**
- **100G (3 OUNCES) BUTTER, EXTRA, MELTED**
- **1 TABLESPOON FINELY GRATED ORANGE RIND**
- **1 TABLESPOON FINELY GRATED LEMON RIND**
- **2 TABLESPOONS DEMERARA SUGAR, EXTRA**
- **250G (8 OUNCES) FIG JAM**
- **5 FIGS (300G), TORN IN HALF**

1 Combine yeast, caster sugar and milk in a large bowl; cover, stand in a warm place for 10 minutes or until frothy. Add egg yolks, butter, the water, flour and salt; stir until combined. Transfer dough to a lightly floured surface; knead for 10 minutes or until smooth and elastic. Place dough in a lightly oiled large bowl; cover, stand in a warm place for 1 hour or until doubled in size.

2 Process three-quarters of the hazelnuts for 1 minute or until finely ground. Combine ground nuts in a small bowl with demerara sugar and mixed spice.

3 Preheat oven to 200°C/400°F. Grease a large oven tray.

4 Lightly flour a large piece of baking paper; roll dough out on paper into a 25cm x 45cm (10-inch x 18-inch) rectangle. Lift dough on paper onto tray, cover with plastic wrap; refrigerate for 1 hour or until firmed slightly. (This will assist with shaping the twist.)

5 Combine 80g (2½ ounces) of extra melted butter with the citrus rinds in a small bowl. Brush butter mixture over dough, leaving a 1cm (½-inch) border; top with ground hazelnut mixture. Firmly roll dough up from one long side, using the baking paper as a guide. Using a sharp knife, cut the roll in half lengthways. Turn the halves, cut-side out on the baking paper, then twist together. Form the twisted lengths into a ring, pressing the two ends together to join.

6 Transfer the ring, carefully lifting it with the baking paper, onto the oven tray. Brush with remaining extra melted butter; sprinkle with extra demerara sugar.

7 Bake for 10 minutes. Reduce oven temperature to 180°C/350°F; bake for a further 35 minutes or until golden and hollow sounding when tapped. Transfer twist to a wire rack to cool. Serve topped with remaining halved hazelnuts, fig jam and fresh figs.

tip This recipe is best made on the day of serving.

QUATTRO FORMAGGI PIZZA

PREP + COOK TIME **30 MINUTES (+ STANDING)** SERVES **4**

**100G (3 OUNCES)
    BOCCONCINI, SLICED THINLY**
**½ CUP (40G) FINELY
    GRATED PARMESAN**
**½ CUP (50G) COARSELY
    GRATED FONTINA CHEESE**
**50G (1½ OUNCES)
    GORGONZOLA CHEESE,
    CRUMBLED**
4 SPRIGS FRESH THYME

PIZZA DOUGH
**1½ CUPS (225G) '00' FLOUR,
    BREAD FLOUR OR PLAIN
    (ALL-PURPOSE) FLOUR**
1 TEASPOON (4G) DRIED YEAST
**1 TEASPOON CASTER
    (SUPERFINE) SUGAR**
1 TEASPOON FINE TABLE SALT
1 TABLESPOON OLIVE OIL
**½ CUP (125ML) WARM WATER,
    APPROXIMATELY**

1 Make pizza dough.
2 Preheat oven to 240°C/475°F. Oil a pizza tray or oven tray; place in heated oven.
3 Roll dough into a 35cm (14-inch) round. Place on tray.
4 Top pizza base with bocconcini; sprinkle with remaining cheeses.
5 Bake for 15 minutes or until base is browned and crisp. Served topped with thyme.

pizza dough Combine flour, yeast, sugar and salt in a medium bowl; make a well in the centre. Stir in oil and enough of the water to mix to a soft dough. Knead dough on a floured surface for 10 minutes or until smooth and elastic. Place dough in a large oiled bowl, cover; stand in a warm place for 1 hour or until dough doubles in size. Turn dough onto a floured surface; knead until smooth.

tip For individual servings, divide the dough into four pieces. Roll each piece on floured surface into 10cm x 20cm (4-inch x 8-inch) slipper shapes.

2 MEALS
FROM 1

2 MEALS ☆ FROM 1

photograph page 186

1. SLOW-COOKED GREEK LAMB WITH CHILLI GARLIC BROCCOLINI

PREP + COOK TIME 5½ HOURS SERVES 4

2 MEDIUM BROWN ONIONS (300G), CUT INTO WEDGES

8 CLOVES GARLIC, UNPEELED, BRUISED

4 BAY LEAVES

6 X 10CM (4-INCH) SPRIGS FRESH ROSEMARY

2 X 1.6KG (3¼-POUND) LAMB SHOULDERS ON THE BONE

1 TABLESPOON EXTRA VIRGIN OLIVE OIL

2 TEASPOONS DRIED OREGANO LEAVES

1 CUP (250ML) CHICKEN STOCK

1 MEDIUM LEMON (140G), CUT INTO WEDGES

CHILLI GARLIC BROCCOLINI

½ CUP (125ML) WATER

2 LONG FRESH RED CHILLIES, HALVED LENGTHWAYS

2 CLOVES GARLIC, CRUSHED

20G (¾ OUNCE) BUTTER

400G (12½ OUNCES) BROCCOLINI, TRIMMED

1 Preheat oven to 160°C/325°F. Oil the base of two large shallow-sided oven trays. Divide onion, garlic, bay leaves, rosemary, then lamb between trays. Rub lamb with oil; sprinkle with oregano. Season well.

2 Pour stock into base of trays; cover trays tightly with foil. Roast lamb for 5 hours.

3 Increase oven to 200°C/400°F. Remove foil from lamb, skim fat from the liquid; spoon pan juices over lamb.

4 Roast lamb, uncovered, for a further 10 minutes or until juices are reduced and lamb is browned. Reserve one lamb shoulder for Recipe 2, page 185 (see tips).

5 Meanwhile, make chilli garlic broccolini.

6 Serve lamb and pan juices with chilli garlic broccolini and lemon wedges.

chilli garlic broccolini Bring the water, chilli, garlic and butter to the boil in a large saucepan over medium heat. Season. Add broccolini; cook, covered, for 4 minutes or until broccolini is tender and water is almost evaporated. Reserve one-third (150g) of the broccolini for Recipe 2, page 185. Cover and refrigerate.

tips It's easier to coarsely shred the lamb for Recipe 2 while it is still warm; you will need 3 cups (420g) coarsely shredded lamb.

This recipe is not suitable to freeze.

serving suggestion Serve with roast potato wedges or mash.

photograph page 187

2.SLOW-COOKED
LAMB &
ROSEMARY PASTA

PREP + COOK TIME **20 MINUTES** SERVES **4**

400G (12½ OUNCES) CASARECCE OR FUSILLI PASTA
2 TABLESPOONS EXTRA VIRGIN OLIVE OIL
2 LONG FRESH RED CHILLIES, SLICED THINLY
2 CLOVES GARLIC, CRUSHED
1 TABLESPOON FINELY CHOPPED FRESH ROSEMARY LEAVES
3 CUPS (420G) RESERVED SHREDDED SLOW-COOKED LAMB (RECIPE 1, PAGE 184)
150G (4½ OUNCES) RESERVED CHILLI GARLIC BROCCOLINI (RECIPE 1, PAGE 184), CUT INTO 3 CROSSWAYS
½ CUP LOOSELY PACKED FRESH FLAT-LEAF PARSLEY LEAVES, CHOPPED
1 CUP (80G) FINELY GRATED PARMESAN

1 Cook pasta in a large saucepan of boiling salted water until just tender. Drain, reserving ½ cup (125ml) cooking liquid. Return pasta to pan; cover to keep warm.

2 Meanwhile, heat oil in a large non-stick frying pan over medium heat; cook chilli, garlic and rosemary, stirring for 30 seconds or until fragrant.

3 Add shredded lamb to pan; cook, stirring, for a further 1 minute or until lamb is hot. Stir in pasta, broccolini mixture, parsley, reserved cooking liquid and half the parmesan.

4 Serve pasta with remaining parmesan.

tips The starch in the reserved pasta water helps to thicken the sauce and coat the pasta.

This recipe is not suitable to freeze.

**1. SLOW-COOKED GREEK LAMB
WITH CHILLI GARLIC BROCCOLINI**
(See recipe page 184)

**2. SLOW-COOKED LAMB
& ROSEMARY PASTA**

(See recipe page 185)

photograph page 190

1. MIDDLE-EASTERN BEEF WITH HERB COUSCOUS

PREP + COOK TIME 40 MINUTES SERVES 4

- 2 TABLESPOONS EXTRA VIRGIN OLIVE OIL
- 1 MEDIUM BROWN ONION (150G), CHOPPED FINELY
- 2 CLOVES GARLIC, CHOPPED FINELY
- 1 TABLESPOON BAHARAT SPICE MIX
- 1 TEASPOON GROUND ALLSPICE
- 1KG (2 POUNDS) MINCED (GROUND) BEEF
- ½ CUP (125ML) CHICKEN STOCK
- 2 TEASPOONS FINELY GRATED LEMON RIND
- 2 TABLESPOONS LEMON JUICE
- 1 CUP LOOSELY PACKED FRESH CORIANDER (CILANTRO) LEAVES, CHOPPED
- 2 CUPS (400G) COUSCOUS
- 2 CUPS (500ML) BOILING WATER
- 1 CUP LOOSELY PACKED FRESH FLAT-LEAF PARSLEY LEAVES, CHOPPED
- 100G (3 OUNCES) FETTA, CRUMBLED
- ½ CUP LOOSELY PACKED MICRO HERBS

YOGHURT SAUCE

- 1 CUP (280G) GREEK YOGHURT
- ½ TEASPOON BAHARAT SPICE MIX
- 1 TABLESPOON LEMON JUICE
- 2 TABLESPOONS FINELY CHOPPED FRESH MINT

PARSLEY OIL

- 2 TABLESPOONS EXTRA VIRGIN OLIVE OIL
- 1 TABLESPOON FINELY CHOPPED FRESH FLAT-LEAF PARSLEY
- 1 TABLESPOON LEMON JUICE

1 Heat half the oil in a large non-stick frying pan over medium heat; cook onion, garlic and spices, stirring, for 5 minutes or until softened. Remove from pan.

2 Cook beef in same pan, in batches, stirring, to break up any lumps, for 7 minutes or until browned and crisp. Return onion mixture to pan; add stock. Cook, stirring, for 5 minutes or until liquid is reduced. Stir in rind, juice and half the coriander; season. Remove from heat.

Reserve 2 cups (400g) of the beef mixture for Recipe 2, page 189; cover, refrigerate. Cover beef mixture in pan to keep warm.

3 Place couscous and remaining oil in a large heatproof bowl with the boiling water. Cover; stand for 5 minutes or until water is absorbed. Fluff with a fork; season. Stir in parsley and remaining coriander. Reserve 1 cup (150g) of the herb couscous for Recipe 2, page 189; cover, refrigerate.

4 Meanwhile, make yoghurt sauce and parsley oil.

5 Serve beef mixture on couscous; top with fetta, yoghurt sauce and herbs. Drizzle with parsley oil.

yoghurt sauce Stir ingredients in a small bowl; season. Reserve ½ cup (140g) sauce for Recipe 2, page 189; cover, refrigerate.

parsley oil Stir ingredients in a small bowl; season.

tip *The beef mixture is suitable to freeze for up to 1 month at the end of step 2.*

photograph page 191

2. MIDDLE-EASTERN BEEF FILLO CIGARS

PREP + COOK TIME **45 MINUTES** SERVES **4**

- 2 CUPS (400G) RESERVED BEEF MIXTURE (RECIPE 1, PAGE 188)
- 1 CUP (150G) RESERVED HERB COUSCOUS (RECIPE 1, PAGE 188)
- 100G (3 OUNCES) FETTA, CRUMBLED
- 2 TABLESPOONS FINELY CHOPPED FRESH FLAT-LEAF PARSLEY
- 12 SHEETS FILLO PASTRY
- 100G (3 OUNCES) BUTTER, MELTED
- 1 TABLESPOON BLACK SESAME SEEDS
- ½ CUP (140G) RESERVED YOGHURT SAUCE (RECIPE 1, PAGE 188)

1 Preheat oven to 200°C/400°F. Line two large oven trays with baking paper.
2 Combine beef mixture, herb couscous, fetta and parsley in a large bowl; season to taste.
3 Place one pastry sheet on a work surface and cover remaining sheets with baking paper then a damp tea-towel to prevent drying out. Lightly brush sheet with butter, then fold in half widthways. Spoon ¼ cup of couscous mixture along one long edge. Fold in 4cm (1½ inches) of the short edges from both ends, then roll up tightly, forming a cigar shape. Place on tray. Repeat with remaining pastry and filling.
4 Brush cigars with remaining butter; sprinkle with seeds. Bake for 20 minutes or until golden. Serve with yoghurt sauce.

tips Cigars can be filled and rolled up to 4 hours ahead. Cover with baking paper and a slightly damp tea-towel; refrigerate until ready to bake.

Cigars can be frozen for up to 1 month at the end of step 3. Thaw overnight in the fridge before baking.

**1. MIDDLE-EASTERN BEEF
WITH HERB COUSCOUS**

(See recipe page 188)

**2. MIDDLE-EASTERN BEEF
FILLO CIGARS**
(See recipe page 189)

photograph page 194

1. ALMOND & SAGE SOURDOUGH ROAST CHICKEN

PREP + COOK TIME **2 HOURS** SERVES **4**

1 CUP (160G) ROASTED ALMOND KERNELS, CHOPPED COARSELY

8 FRESH SAGE LEAVES

2 TEASPOONS FINELY GRATED LEMON RIND

3 CLOVES GARLIC, CHOPPED COARSELY

½ CUP (125ML) OLIVE OIL

2 X 1.8KG (3½-POUND) WHOLE CHICKENS

½ BUNCH CELERY (750G), PALE INNER LEAVES RESERVED

600G (1¼-POUND) LOAF SOURDOUGH, HALVED HORIZONTALLY

4 BABY PARSNIPS (480G), HALVED LENGTHWAYS

1 BUNCH (400G) BABY HEIRLOOM CARROTS, TRIMMED LEAVING 1CM (½-INCH) STALK

2 CUPS (500ML) CHICKEN STOCK

40G (1½ OUNCES) BUTTER, CHOPPED

ALMOND GREMOLATA

¾ CUP (120G) FINELY CHOPPED ROASTED ALMOND KERNELS

1 CLOVE GARLIC, CRUSHED

1 TABLESPOON FINELY GRATED LEMON RIND

½ CUP FINELY CHOPPED FRESH FLAT-LEAF PARSLEY

1 Preheat oven to 200°C/400°F. Oil a large baking dish.

2 Blend or process almonds, sage, rind, garlic and ¼ cup oil until a rough paste forms; season.

3 Pat chickens dry with paper towel. Evenly spread almond mixture between the skin and the breast and tops of the legs of each chicken. Place both chickens into baking dish; season.

4 Place celery around chickens. Tear bottom half of sourdough into 4cm (1½-inch) pieces. Place bread on chickens and celery; drizzle with remaining oil. Reserve top half of sourdough for Recipe 2, page 193.

5 Place parsnip, carrot and stock in another large baking dish; top with butter. Season. Roast chickens and vegetables for 1¼ hours or until chickens are cooked through. Transfer chickens, breast-side down, to a tray; cover with foil. Stand for 15 minutes. Roast vegetables for a further 20 minutes or until golden and tender.

6 Make almond gremolata.

7 Serve one chicken with sourdough and vegetables, sprinkled with almond gremolata. Keep remaining chicken for Recipe 2.

almond gremolata Combine ingredients in a small bowl. Reserve ¼ cup gremolata for Recipe 2, page 193; cover, refrigerate.

tip This recipe is not suitable to freeze.

photograph page 195

2. TAGLIATELLE WITH CRISP CHICKEN & SAGE PANGRATTATO

PREP + COOK TIME **30 MINUTES** SERVES **4**

- 300G (9½ OUNCES) RESERVED SOURDOUGH BREAD (RECIPE 1, PAGE 192)
- 8 FRESH SAGE LEAVES, CHOPPED
- ½ CUP (125ML) EXTRA VIRGIN OLIVE OIL
- 500G (1 POUND) TAGLIATELLE PASTA
- 4½ CUPS (800G) COARSELY SHREDDED RESERVED CHICKEN (RECIPE 1, PAGE 192)
- 2 CLOVES GARLIC, CRUSHED
- 100G (3 OUNCES) BUTTER, CHOPPED
- ¼ CUP (50G) RESERVED ALMOND GREMOLATA (RECIPE 1, PAGE 192)

1 Pulse bread and sage in a processor until coarse crumbs form. Heat ¼ cup of the oil in a large frying pan over high heat; cook crumbs, stirring occasionally, for 3 minutes or until golden. Drain on paper towel; season to taste. Wipe out pan with paper towel.

2 Meanwhile, cook pasta in a large saucepan of boiling salted water until just tender. Reserve ½ cup (125ml) cooking liquid; drain.

3 Add 2 tablespoons of the remaining oil to same frying pan over high heat. Add shredded chicken and garlic; cook, stirring occasionally, for 5 minutes or until chicken is golden and hot. Add butter; stir until just melted.

4 Working quickly, add hot pasta immediately to chicken mixture in pan with almond gremolata, remaining oil and reserved cooking water; toss until well combined. Season to taste; add half the crumbs, toss gently. Serve sprinkled with remaining crumbs.

tip This recipes is best made close to serving, as the breadcrumbs soak up the liquid while it stands. This recipe is not suitable to freeze.

1. ALMOND & SAGE SOURDOUGH
ROAST CHICKEN
(See recipe page 192)

**2. TAGLIATELLE WITH CRISP CHICKEN
& SAGE PANGRATTATO**

(See recipe page 193)

photograph page 198

1. ROAST WINTER VEGETABLES WITH CREAMY POLENTA

PREP + COOK TIME **1½ HOURS** SERVES **4**

- **2 MEDIUM KOHLRABI (1KG), TRIMMED, QUARTERED**
- **2 MEDIUM TURNIPS (460G), QUARTERED**
- **2 MEDIUM KUMARA (ORANGE SWEET POTATOES) (800G), QUARTERED LENGTHWAYS**
- **400G (12½ OUNCES) BABY HEIRLOOM CARROTS, TRIMMED**
- **2 BULBS GARLIC, HALVED CROSSWAYS**
- **¼ CUP (60ML) EXTRA VIRGIN OLIVE OIL**
- **2 TABLESPOONS RED WINE VINEGAR**
- **1 CUP (220G) WALNUT AND PARSLEY PESTO**
- **120G (4 OUNCES) HARD ASHED GOAT'S CHEESE, SHAVED**
- **¼ CUP LOOSELY PACKED FRESH FLAT-LEAF PARSLEY LEAVES**

CREAMY POLENTA
- **1 LITRE (4 CUPS) MILK**
- **1 LITRE (4 CUPS) VEGETABLE STOCK**
- **2 CUPS (340G) POLENTA**
- **1 CUP (80G) FINELY GRATED PARMESAN**
- **125G (4 OUNCES) MASCARPONE**

1 Preheat oven to 200°C/400°F. Line two large oven trays with baking paper.

2 Place vegetables and garlic in a large bowl; drizzle with oil and vinegar. Season; toss to coat. Divide vegetables between trays. Roast vegetables for 40 minutes or until garlic is tender. Remove garlic; cover to keep warm. Roast remaining vegetables for a further 30 minutes or until tender and golden.

3 Meanwhile, 20 minutes before vegetables are cooked, make mascarpone polenta.

4 Pour mascarpone polenta over a large serving platter; top with half the vegetables and three-quarters of the pesto. Reserve remaining vegetables and pesto for Recipe 2, page 197.

5 Serve polenta and vegetables immediately, topped with goat's cheese and parsley.

creamy polenta Bring the milk and stock to the boil in a large saucepan. Gradually add polenta, whisking constantly, until thickened. Reduce heat to low; simmer, stirring often, for 15 minutes or until smooth. Stir in parmesan; season. Pour half the polenta into a greased and baking-paper-lined 15cm (6-inch) square cake pan for Recipe 2, page 197. Fold mascarpone through remaining hot polenta.

tips It is easier to pour the reserved portion of creamy polenta for Recipe 2 into the lined cake pan while it is still warm.

This recipe is not suitable to freeze.

photograph page 199

2. BUBBLE & SQUEAK WITH MAPLE BACON & POLENTA CHIPS

PREP + COOK TIME **1 HOUR (+ REFRIGERATION)** SERVES **4**

- 1 CUP (250G) RESERVED POLENTA IN CAKE PAN (RECIPE 1, PAGE 196)
- 600G (1¼ POUNDS) RESERVED ROAST VEGETABLES (RECIPE 1, PAGE 196)
- 40G (1½ OUNCES) BUTTER
- 8 RINDLESS BACON SLICES (500G)
- 2 TABLESPOONS MAPLE SYRUP
- 2 TABLESPOONS LIGHT BROWN SUGAR
- 1 TABLESPOON OLIVE OIL
- 1 RED WITLOF (BELGIAN ENDIVE) (125G), LEAVES SEPARATED
- ¼ CUP (65G) RESERVED PESTO (RECIPE 1, PAGE 196)

1 Preheat oven to 220°C/425°F. Line two large oven trays with baking paper.

2 Press reserved polenta evenly over base of the baking-paper-lined pan. (If polenta has cooled, reheat it gently until soft enough to spread into the pan.) Cover; refrigerate for 1 hour or until firm.

3 Meanwhile, finely chop the roast vegetables; transfer to a medium bowl. Mash vegetables until thoroughly combined; season to taste. Divide into 4 portions.

4 Melt butter in a medium non-stick frying pan over medium heat. Add vegetable mixture portions to pan, pressing out evenly. Reduce heat to low; cook for 3 minutes or until browned. Turn over in sections to cook other side (you will not be able to turn this over in one whole piece); press down to compress mixture. Continue to cook and turn for further 5 minutes or until browned. Remove from heat; cover to keep warm.

5 Meanwhile, combine bacon, maple syrup and sugar in a medium bowl until combined. Spread evenly on one tray.

6 Turn polenta out of pan; cut in half, then each half into six fingers. Spread evenly on second tray; drizzle with oil.

7 Bake polenta and bacon for 25 minutes, turning halfway, or until polenta is lightly golden and bacon is dark and glossy.

8 Carefully slide bubble and squeak onto a serving platter; top with witlof, polenta chips and bacon. Drizzle with pesto. Top with parsley, if you like.

tip This recipe is not suitable to freeze.

1. ROAST WINTER VEGETABLES
WITH CREAMY POLENTA
(See recipe page 196)

2. BUBBLE & SQUEAK WITH
MAPLE BACON & POLENTA CHIPS
(See recipe page 197)

photograph page 202

1. PORK & CIDER SKEWERS WITH BLUE CHEESE SLAW

PREP + COOK TIME **45 MINUTES (+ REFRIGERATION)** SERVES **4**

1⅓ CUPS (330ML) APPLE CIDER

3 CLOVES GARLIC, CRUSHED

¼ CUP (90G) HONEY

2 TEASPOONS FINELY CHOPPED FRESH ROSEMARY

1.6KG (3¼ POUNDS) TRIMMED PORK NECK, CUT INTO 5CM (2-INCH) PIECES

8 SMALL RED APPLES (1KG), SOME LEFT WHOLE AND SOME HALVED

½ MEDIUM RED CABBAGE (750G), SHREDDED FINELY

4 GREEN ONIONS (SCALLIONS), SLICED THINLY LENGTHWAYS

50G (1½ OUNCES) BLUE CHEESE, CRUMBLED

BLUE CHEESE SAUCE

1 CUP (240G) SOUR CREAM

150G (4½ OUNCES) BLUE CHEESE, CRUMBLED

⅓ CUP (80ML) LEMON JUICE

3 GREEN ONIONS (SCALLIONS), SLICED THINLY

1 Combine cider, garlic, honey, rosemary and pork in a large bowl. Cover; refrigerate for at least 1 hour or overnight.

2 Preheat oven to 220°C/425°F. Grease and line two large oven trays with baking paper.

3 Thread half the pork and all the apple alternately onto 8 large skewers; season. Place on one tray. Place remaining pork on second tray. Roast both trays for 20 minutes or until pork is just cooked through. Reserve pork pieces for Recipe 2, page 201.

4 Meanwhile, make blue cheese sauce.

5 Combine cabbage and onion in a medium bowl; season. Reserve one-quarter of the slaw mixture for Recipe 2, page 201.

6 Serve skewers with remaining slaw mixture; drizzled with ½ cup (125ml) of the blue cheese sauce. Sprinkle with crumbled cheese.

blue cheese sauce Blend or process sour cream, blue cheese and juice until smooth. Transfer to a bowl; stir in onion. Season to taste. Reserve 1 cup for Recipe 2, page 201.

tips *You will need 8 large metal skewers for this recipe.*

This recipe is not suitable to freeze.

serving suggestion *Serve with slices of crusty bread or roast potatoes.*

photograph page 203

2. STICKY PORK ROLLS WITH RED SLAW

PREP + COOK TIME **20 MINUTES** SERVES **4**

2 TABLESPOONS OLIVE OIL

750G (1½ POUNDS) RESERVED PORK, SHREDDED (RECIPE 1, PAGE 200)

¼ CUP (90G) HONEY

4 LONG BREAD ROLLS (320G)

2 CUPS (160G) RESERVED SLAW MIXTURE (RECIPE 1, PAGE 200)

1 CUP (250ML) RESERVED BLUE CHEESE SAUCE (RECIPE 1, PAGE 200)

1 Preheat oven to 120°C/250°F.

2 Heat oil in a large frying pan over high heat; cook shredded pork, stirring occasionally, for 5 minutes or until browned. Add honey; cook, stirring occasionally, for a further 2 minutes or until pork is golden and coated. Season to taste.

3 Meanwhile, warm bread rolls in oven for 5 minutes or until heated through. (Alternatively, warm bread rolls in the microwave on HIGH (100%) power for 20 seconds.)

4 Cut rolls in half lengthways; divide pork and slaw mixture between rolls. Drizzle with sauce.

tip This recipe is not suitable to freeze.

1. PORK & CIDER SKEWERS
WITH BLUE CHEESE SLAW
(See recipe page 200)

**2. STICKY PORK ROLLS
WITH RED SLAW**
(See recipe page 201)

photograph page 206

1. LAMB SHANKS WITH MASH & SILVER BEET

PREP + COOK TIME **3½ HOURS** SERVES **4**

¼ CUP (60ML) OLIVE OIL

6 LAMB SHANKS (2.25KG)

1 LARGE BROWN ONION (200G), CHOPPED COARSELY

5 CLOVES GARLIC, PEELED

2 TABLESPOONS TOMATO PASTE

1½ CUPS (375ML) DRY RED WINE

2 CUPS (500ML) BEEF STOCK

400G (12½ OUNCES) CANNED DICED TOMATOES

1 TABLESPOON SUGAR

4 SPRIGS FRESH ROSEMARY

1KG (2 POUNDS) SILVER BEET (SWISS CHARD), STALKS TRIMMED, LEAVES SHREDDED

MASH

1.4KG (2¾ POUNDS) FLOURY POTATOES, PEELED, HALVED

100G (3 OUNCES) BUTTER, CHOPPED

½ CUP (125ML) THICKENED CREAM, WARMED

1 Preheat oven to 150°C/300°F.

2 Heat 1 tablespoon of the oil in a large flameproof casserole dish; cook lamb, in two batches, for 5 minutes or until browned all over. Remove from dish.

3 Add onion and 3 crushed garlic cloves to same dish; cook, stirring, until onion softens. Add paste; cook, stirring, for 2 minutes. Stir in wine; bring to the boil. Boil, uncovered, for 5 minutes or until reduced by half.

4 Return lamb to dish with stock, tomatoes, sugar and rosemary. Cover; roast for 2 hours. Remove lid; bake a further 1 hour or until lamb is tender.

5 Meanwhile, make mash.

6 Heat remaining oil in a large frying pan on medium heat, add thinly sliced remaining garlic; cook, stirring, for 1 minute. Add silver beet; cook, stirring, for 3 minutes or until wilted.

7 Reserve 2 of the shanks and 1 cup (250ml) of the cooking liquid for Recipe 2, page 205.

8 Serve remaining shanks drizzled with the remaining cooking liquid, creamy mash and silver beet.

mash Place potato in a large saucepan of cold salted water. Cover; bring to the boil over high heat. Cook for 10 minutes or until just tender. Using a slotted spoon, remove two-fifths (400g) of the potato from water; place in a bowl, cover, refrigerate for Recipe 2, page 205. Continue cooking remaining potato until tender. Drain, return to pan over low heat; cook for 1 minute or until excess moisture has evaporated. Mash with butter and cream until smooth.

tip This recipe is suitable to freeze for up to 3 months at the end of step 4.

photograph page 207

2. LAMB POT PIES WITH MUSHY PEAS

PREP + COOK TIME **25 MINUTES** SERVES **4**

1 TABLESPOON OLIVE OIL

2 RESERVED LAMB SHANKS, MEAT SHREDDED (RECIPE 1, PAGE 204)

1 MEDIUM CARROT (120G), CHOPPED COARSELY

1 TABLESPOON GRAVY POWDER

1 CUP (250ML) RESERVED COOKING LIQUID (RECIPE 1, PAGE 204)

½ CUP (125ML) WATER

400G (12½ OUNCES) CANNED LENTILS, DRAINED, RINSED

½ CUP (60G) FROZEN PEAS

500G (1 POUND) RESERVED PAR-BOILED POTATOES, SLICED THINLY (RECIPE 1, PAGE 204)

50G (1½ OUNCES) BUTTER, MELTED

MUSHY PEAS

90G (3 OUNCES) BUTTER, CHOPPED

4 CUPS (480G) FROZEN PEAS

2 TABLESPOONS FINELY CHOPPED FRESH MINT

2 TEASPOONS CASTER (SUPERFINE) SUGAR

¼ CUP (60ML) LEMON JUICE

1 Preheat oven to 200°C/400°F. Grease four 1¼-cup (310ml) ramekins or ovenproof dishes. Place dishes on an oven tray.

2 Heat oil in a large frying pan over high heat. Add shredded lamb and carrot; cook, stirring, until hot. Add gravy powder; cook, stirring, for 1 minute. Stir in reserved cooking liquid and water; bring to the boil. Boil for 2 minutes. Stir in lentils and peas. Divide mixture between ramekins.

3 Arrange sliced potato over lamb mixture, brushing with melted butter between layers. Bake for 20 minutes until potato is golden.

4 Meanwhile, make mushy peas.

5 Serve pies with mushy peas.

mushy peas Melt butter in a medium saucepan over medium heat; cook peas, mint and sugar for 6 minutes, stirring, until tender. Using a stick blender; puree pea mixture until combined. Stir in juice; season to taste.

tip This recipe is suitable to freeze for up to 1 month.

serving suggestion Serve with a mixed leaf salad and tomato sauce (ketchup).

1. LAMB SHANKS
WITH MASH & SILVER BEET
(See recipe page 204)

**2. LAMB POT PIES
WITH MUSHY PEAS**
(See recipe page 205)

photograph page 212

1. SLOW-COOKED
BOLOGNESE

PREP + COOK TIME **2 HOURS** SERVES **4**

1 TABLESPOON OLIVE OIL

1 LARGE BROWN ONION
(200G), CHOPPED FINELY

2 CELERY STALKS (300G),
TRIMMED, CHOPPED

2 LARGE CARROTS (360G),
CHOPPED

100G (3 OUNCES) PROSCIUTTO,
CHOPPED FINELY

2 CLOVES GARLIC, CRUSHED

1KG (2 POUNDS) MINCED
(GROUND) PORK AND VEAL
(SEE TIPS)

¼ CUP (70G) TOMATO PASTE

1 TEASPOON DRIED OREGANO
LEAVES

1 CUP (250ML) DRY RED WINE

700G (1½ POUNDS) BOTTLED
TOMATO PASSATA

2 CUPS (500ML) BEEF STOCK

1 TABLESPOON CHOPPED
FRESH ROSEMARY

2 SPRIGS FRESH THYME

100G (3 OUNCE) BLOCK
PARMESAN, RIND REMOVED
AND RESERVED

400G (12½ OUNCES)
SPAGHETTI

1 Heat oil in a large saucepan over high heat; cook onion, celery, carrot, prosciutto and garlic, stirring, for 5 minutes or until onion is soft. Add mince; cook, stirring, to break up lumps, for 10 minutes or until browned.

2 Stir in paste and oregano; cook, stirring, for 2 minutes. Add wine, bring to the boil; simmer, uncovered, for 4 minutes or until reduced by half. Stir in passata, stock, rosemary, thyme and parmesan rind; bring to boil. Reduce heat to low, cover with a lid; simmer for 1½ hours, stirring occasionally, until thickened. Season. Remove and discard parmesan rind from sauce.

3 Shave remaining parmesan; cover, refrigerate.

4 Meanwhile, cook spaghetti in a large saucepan of boiling salted water for 8 minutes or until just tender; drain.

5 Reserve 2 cups of the bolognese sauce for Recipe 2, page 211.

6 Serve spaghetti with bolognese sauce; sprinkle with shaved parmesan and fresh oregano leaves, if you like.

tips *Some butchers sell a minced (ground) pork and veal mixture. If it is not available as a mixture, buy 500g (1 pound) of each. You can also use minced beef or a combination of minced beef and pork and veal, if you prefer.*

This recipe is suitable to freeze at the end of step 2.

photograph page 213

2.STOVETOP "BAKED" EGGS

PREP + COOK TIME **25 MINUTES** SERVES **4**

1 CURED CHORIZO SAUSAGE
   (100G), SLICED
2 CUPS RESERVED
   BOLOGNESE SAUCE
   (RECIPE 1, PAGE 210)
400G (12½ OUNCES) CANNED
   CHERRY TOMATOES
½ TEASPOON DRIED
   CHILLI FLAKES
400G (12½ OUNCES)
   CANNED FOUR-BEAN MIX,
   DRAINED, RINSED
2 TABLESPOONS CHOPPED
   FRESH FLAT-LEAF PARSLEY
100G (3 OUNCES) BABY
   SPINACH LEAVES
4 EGGS
100G (3 OUNCES) PERSIAN
   FETTA, CRUMBLED

1 Cook chorizo in a large frying pan over medium-high heat, turning occasionally, for 2 minutes or until browned. Add bolognese sauce, tomatoes and chilli; bring to the boil. Stir in beans, parsley and half the spinach; cook, stirring, for 3 minutes or until beans are hot. Season to taste.
2 Using the back of a spoon, make four small indents in the mixture. Crack an egg into each indent. Cook, covered, for 5 minutes, or until eggs are just set or cooked to your liking.
3 Serve topped with remaining spinach and fetta.

tips You can adjust or omit the amount of chilli flakes depending on how much heat you like.

This recipe is not suitable to freeze.

serving suggestion
Serve with char-grilled sourdough bread slices.

1. SLOW-COOKED
BOLOGNESE
(See recipe page 210)

2. STOVETOP
"BAKED" EGGS
(See recipe page 211)

2 MEALS ☆ FROM 1

photograph page 216

1. BUTTERFLIED ROAST CHICKEN & BRAISED LEEKS

PREP + COOK TIME **1¾ HOURS** SERVES **4**

- **1.5KG (3 POUNDS) SEBAGO POTATOES, CUT INTO LARGE PIECES**
- **¼ CUP (60ML) OLIVE OIL**
- **100G (3 OUNCES) BUTTER, SOFTENED**
- **2 TABLESPOONS FINELY CHOPPED FRESH FLAT-LEAF PARSLEY**
- **1 TABLESPOON FRESH THYME LEAVES**
- **1 TABLESPOON FINELY GRATED LEMON RIND**
- **2 X 1.8KG (3½-POUND) WHOLE CHICKENS**
- **4 SMALL LEEKS (1KG), TRIMMED**
- **2 CLOVES GARLIC, BRUISED**
- **2 SPRIGS FRESH THYME**
- **1 CUP (250ML) CHICKEN STOCK**

GREMOLATA DRESSING
- **1 CUP LOOSELY PACKED FRESH FLAT-LEAF PARSLEY LEAVES, CHOPPED**
- **1 SMALL CLOVE GARLIC, CHOPPED FINELY**
- **2 TABLESPOONS FINELY CHOPPED CORNICHONS**
- **⅓ CUP (80ML) OLIVE OIL**
- **1 TABLESPOON LEMON JUICE**

1 Preheat oven to 200°C/400°F.
2 Place potatoes in a saucepan of salted cold water over high heat; bring to the boil. Boil, covered, for 10 minutes or until just tender. Drain in a colander; toss lightly to rough the edges. Toss potatoes in a large shallow baking dish with 2 tablespoons of the oil; season well. Roast for 20 minutes.
3 Combine butter, parsley, thyme leaves and rind in a bowl; season.
4 To butterfly chickens, cut along either side of backbones with kitchen scissors; discard backbones. Open chickens out; press firmly on breast to flatten. Tuck wing tips under body. Carefully loosen skin of chickens over the breasts. Push the butter mixture between the skin and the breast and over the drumsticks and thighs. Place chickens on a large oven tray (or two small oven trays). Roast chickens on separate shelf with potatoes for a further 45 minutes or until chicken is cooked through and potatoes are golden brown. Reserve one chicken and 2 cups (280g) coarsely chopped potatoes for Recipe 2, page 215; cover, refrigerate.
5 Meanwhile, place leeks in a small baking dish with garlic, thyme sprigs and remaining oil; season. Drizzle with stock; cover tray with foil. Roast for 30 minutes. Remove foil; roast a further 10 minutes or until golden and tender. Reserve one leek for Recipe 2; transfer to a plate, cover, refrigerate. Halve remaining leeks lengthways.
6 Meanwhile, make gremolata dressing.
7 Serve chicken with potatoes, leeks and gremolata dressing.
gremolata dressing Combine ingredients in a bowl; season.

tip *This recipe is not suitable to freeze.*

photograph page 217

2.CHICKEN, POTATO & LEEK POT PIES

PREP + COOK TIME **40 MINUTES (+ REFRIGERATION)** SERVES **4**

2 TABLESPOONS OLIVE OIL

2 BACON SLICES (160G), TRIMMED, CHOPPED

1 RESERVED BRAISED LEEK, SLICED (RECIPE 1, PAGE 214)

1 CLOVE GARLIC, CRUSHED

1 TABLESPOON PLAIN (ALL-PURPOSE) FLOUR

2 CUPS (500ML) CHICKEN STOCK

¾ CUP (180ML) POURING CREAM

3 CUPS (300G) COARSELY SHREDDED RESERVED ROAST CHICKEN (RECIPE 1, PAGE 214)

2 CUPS (280G) COARSELY CHOPPED ROAST POTATOES (RECIPE 1, PAGE 214)

1 SHEET FROZEN BUTTER PUFF PASTRY, PARTIALLY THAWED

1 EGG, BEATEN LIGHTLY

1 Heat oil in a large non-stick frying pan over medium heat; cook bacon, stirring, for 2 minutes or until browned. Add leek and garlic; cook for a further 1 minute or until garlic is fragrant.

2 Add flour to pan; cook, stirring, for a further 1 minute. Gradually whisk in stock. Whisk until mixture boils and thickens slightly. Whisk in cream; simmer for a further 1 minute. Remove from heat; season to taste.

3 Transfer mixture to a large heatproof bowl, add chicken and potato; toss well to coat. Refrigerate until cold.

4 Preheat oven to 200°C/400°F.

5 Lightly oil four 1¼-cup (300ml) ramekins. Using top of a ramekin as a guide, cut four rounds from pastry. Spoon chicken mixture into ramekins. Place pastry rounds on top of chicken mixture; press with a fork to seal edges. Pierce a small hole in centre of each pastry round; brush with egg.

6 Place ramekins on oven tray; bake for 25 minutes or until golden and puffed.

tips Chicken mixture can be spooned into ramekins and topped with pastry up to 6 hours ahead. Refrigerate until ready to bake.

This recipe is not suitable to freeze.

1. BUTTERFLIED ROAST CHICKEN
& BRAISED LEEKS
(See recipe page 214)

2. CHICKEN, POTATO & LEEK POT PIES
(See recipe page 215)

photograph page 220

1. BRAISED PORK NECK & SHIITAKE MUSHROOMS

PREP + COOK TIME **2½ HOURS (+ STANDING)** SERVES **4**

16 (30G) DRIED SHIITAKE MUSHROOMS

1.5KG (3-POUND) PIECE PORK NECK (SCOTCH FILLET ROAST), FAT TRIMMED

2 TABLESPOONS DARK SOY SAUCE

2 TABLESPOONS LIGHT SOY SAUCE

5CM (2-INCH) PIECE FRESH GINGER (25G), CHOPPED COARSELY

2 CLOVES GARLIC, CHOPPED

1 STICK LEMON GRASS, CHOPPED COARSLEY

4 KAFFIR LIME LEAVES

2 TABLESPOONS BROWN SUGAR

2 WHOLE STAR ANISE

1 LITRE (4 CUPS) CHICKEN STOCK

500G (1 POUND) FRESH RICE NOODLES

1 CUP LOOSELY PACKED FRESH CORIANDER (CILANTRO) LEAVES

1 Place mushrooms in a small bowl; cover with warm water. Stand for 30 minutes.

2 Place pork, soy sauces, ginger, garlic, lemon grass, lime leaves, sugar, star anise, drained mushrooms and stock in a saucepan just large enough to hold the pork. Bring to the boil. Reduce heat to low; simmer, covered, for 2 hours, turning occasionally (liquid won't cover pork completely).

3 Cook noodles in a large saucepan of simmering water for 2 minutes; drain.

4 Transfer pork to a plate; cover, stand for 5 minutes. Discard star anise. Reserve 300g (9½ ounces) pork, 1 cup (250ml) cooking liquid and half the mushrooms for Recipe 2, page 219.

5 Slice remaining pork. Serve on a bed of noodles, drizzled with some of the cooking liquid; top with remaining mushrooms, chilli and coriander.

serving suggestion
Serve with steamed Asian greens such as pak choy, choy sum or gai lan.

photograph page 221

2. PORK & NOODLE SPRING ROLLS

PREP + COOK TIME **1 HOUR** MAKES **20**

300G (9½ OUNCES) RESERVED COOKED PORK (RECIPE 1, PAGE 218)

8 RESERVED MUSHROOMS (RECIPE 1, PAGE 218)

60G (2 OUNCES) DRIED VERMICELLI RICE NOODLES

1 TABLESPOON PEANUT OIL

2 CLOVES GARLIC, CRUSHED

2CM (¾-INCH) PIECE FRESH GINGER (10G), CUT INTO LONG THIN STRIPS

4 GREEN ONIONS (SCALLIONS), SLICED THINLY

2 LONG FRESH RED CHILLIES, SEEDED, CHOPPED FINELY

1 TRIMMED STALK CELERY (100G), CUT INTO LONG THIN STRIPS

2 MEDIUM CARROTS (240G), CUT INTO LONG THIN STRIPS

1 CUP (250ML) RESERVED COOKING LIQUID (RECIPE 1, PAGE 218)

¼ CUP CHOPPED FRESH CORIANDER (CILANTRO)

300G (9½ OUNCE) PACKET SPRING ROLL WRAPPERS

VEGETABLE OIL, FOR DEEP-FRYING

½ TEASPOON SESAME OIL

1 Shred pork and thinly slice mushrooms. Place vermicelli in a medium heatproof bowl; cover with boiling water, stand until just tender, drain.

2 Heat oil in a large frying pan over medium heat; cook garlic, ginger, onion and half the chilli, stirring, for 2 minutes. Add celery and carrot; cook, stirring, for 2 minutes or until softened. Stir in ⅓ cup (80ml) of the reserved cooking liquid, with pork, mushrooms, vermicelli and 2 tablespoons of the coriander; cool.

3 Place a spring roll wrapper on work surface with a point facing you. Place ¼ cup of mixture on lower half of wrapper, fold sides in to the centre and roll up firmly. Moisten end of wrapper with water to secure. Repeat with remaining wrappers and filling.

4 Fill a large saucepan one-third full with oil; heat to 180°C/350°F (or until a cube of bread turns golden in 15 seconds). Deep-fry spring rolls, in batches, until golden brown and heated through. Drain on paper towel.

5 Skim fat solids from remaining reserved cooking liquid. Place liquid in a small saucepan; bring to the boil. Transfer to a small bowl; cool. Stir in remaining chilli, remaining coriander and sesame oil.

6 Serve deep-fried spring rolls with dipping sauce.

tip This recipe is not suitable to freeze.

1. BRAISED PORK NECK
& SHIITAKE MUSHROOMS

(See recipe page 218)

2. PORK & NOODLE SPRING ROLLS
(See recipe page 219)

photograph page 224

1. DUCK RED CURRY

PREP + COOK TIME **35 MINUTES** SERVES **4**

- 1½ PEKING-STYLE ROAST DUCKS (1.8KG) (SEE TIPS)
- 1 TABLESPOON VEGETABLE OIL
- ⅓ CUP (100G) RED CURRY PASTE
- ¼ CUP (65G) GRATED PALM SUGAR
- 2 TABLESPOONS FISH SAUCE
- 1 TABLESPOON TAMARIND CONCENTRATE
- 2 KAFFIR LIME LEAVES, SLICED THINLY
- 3¼ CUPS (800ML) COCONUT MILK
- 1 MEDIUM RED CAPSICUM (BELL PEPPER) (200G), CHOPPED
- 300G (9½ OUNCES) GAI LAN, CUT INTO 5CM (2-INCH) PIECES
- 1 CUP (140G) FROZEN PEAS
- 1 FRESH LONG RED CHILLI, SLICED THINLY
- ¼ CUP LOOSELY PACKED FRESH CORIANDER (CILANTRO) LEAVES
- 1 MEDIUM LIME (90G), CUT INTO WEDGES

1 Remove duck meat using a small sharp knife, keeping skin over breasts intact. Reserve carcass; reserve remaining skin. Slice breast and shred meat from legs. Transfer 2 cups (250g) of the shredded leg meat to a medium bowl; refrigerate meat, skin and carcass for Recipe 2, page 223.

2 Heat oil in a wok or large frying pan over medium heat. Cook curry paste; stirring, for 3 minutes or until fragrant. Add sugar, sauce, tamarind and lime leaves; cook, stirring, for 5 minutes or until mixture darkens slightly, then add the coconut milk and slowly bring to just below the boil. Add vegetables; cook for 3 minutes. Add the remaining duck meat; cook for 2 minutes or until just heated through.

3 Serve curry topped with chilli and coriander, and with lime wedges.

tips *You can buy peking-style roast duck from Asian food stores and some Chinese restaurants. Make sure you specify that the duck is not chopped as the meat and carcass need to be intact for this recipe.*

This recipe is not suitable to freeze.

serving suggestion *Serve with steamed jasmine rice.*

photograph page 225

2. DUCK WONTONS
IN BROTH

PREP + COOK TIME **1 HOUR 50 MINUTES (+ STANDING)** SERVES **4**

8 (16G) DRIED SHIITAKE
  MUSHROOMS
1 LITRE (4 CUPS) BOILING
  WATER
1 MEDIUM RED ONION (170G),
  HALVED CROSSWAYS
1 LARGE BULB GARLIC (100G),
  HALVED CROSSWAYS
6CM (2½-INCH) PIECE FRESH
  GINGER (30G), SLICED
4 LONG FRESH RED CHILLIES
RESERVED DUCK CARCASS
  (RECIPE 1, PAGE 222)
3 STAR ANISE
1 CINNAMON STICK
1 BUNCH CORIANDER
  (CILANTRO) ROOTS AND
  STEMS, LEAVES RESERVED
1.5 LITRES (6 CUPS) CHICKEN
  STOCK
1 TABLESPOON FISH SAUCE
2 TABLESPOONS SOY SAUCE
750G (1½ POUNDS) TAT SOI
2 GREEN ONIONS (SCALLIONS),
  SLICED THINLY LENGTHWAYS
RESERVED DUCK SKIN,
  CRISPED (SEE TIP)

WONTONS

2 CUPS (250G) RESERVED
  SHREDDED DUCK MEAT
  (RECIPE 1, PAGE 222)
227G (7 OUNCES) CANNED
  WATER CHESTNUTS,
  DRAINED, CHOPPED FINELY

2 GREEN ONIONS (SCALLIONS),
  SLICED THINLY
5 CLOVES GARLIC, GRATED
3CM (1¼-INCH) PIECE FRESH
  GINGER (15G), GRATED FINELY
2 TEASPOONS HOISIN SAUCE
2 TEASPOONS SESAME OIL
24 WONTON WRAPPERS

1 Cover mushrooms with boiling water in a heatproof jug. Stand for 30 minutes. Drain; reserve liquid. Finely chop mushrooms; transfer to a medium bowl to use in wontons.

2 Preheat grill (broiler) on high. Grill onion and garlic, cut-side-up, ginger and 2 of the chillies in an ovenproof dish for 15 minutes or until aromatic and charred.

3 Place charred ingredients in a large stock pot with reserved carcass, star anise, cinnamon and coriander roots and stems, stock and reserved mushroom liquid. Bring to the boil. Reduce heat to low; simmer, covered, for 1½ hours.

4 Meanwhile, make wontons.

5 Strain broth through a fine sieve, discarding solids. Transfer to a large saucepan; add sauces, season. Bring to a simmer; cook wontons in soup for 2 minutes or until wrappers have softened and filling is hot.

6 Divide vegetables and wontons between 4 large serving bowls. Divide hot broth between bowls.

7 Seed and thinly slice remaining chillies lengthways. Serve the broth topped with chilli, onion, reserved coriander leaves and crispy duck skin.

wontons Combine duck meat and mushrooms in a bowl with water chestnuts, green onion, garlic, ginger, sauce and oil; season. Place 3 teaspoons filling in the centre of each wrapper; wet edges with water, then bring together and pinch to seal.

tips To crisp duck skin, place on a rack over an oven tray. Bake at 160°C/325°F for 15 minutes or until crisp and fat has rendered from skin.

This recipe is not suitable to freeze.

1. DUCK RED CURRY

(See recipe page 222)

2. DUCK WONTONS IN BROTH

(See recipe page 223)

SWEETS

CHOCOLATE TART
WITH POACHED
PEARS

PREP + COOK TIME **2 HOURS (+ REFRIGERATION, FREEZING & COOLING)**
SERVES **12**

125G (4 OUNCES) COLD BUTTER, CHOPPED

¼ CUP (40G) ICING (CONFECTIONERS') SUGAR

1¼ CUPS (185G) PLAIN (ALL-PURPOSE) FLOUR

1 TABLESPOON DUTCH-PROCESSED COCOA

1 EGG YOLK

1 TABLESPOON CHILLED WATER

400G (12½ OUNCES) DARK CHOCOLATE (50% COCOA), CHOPPED

200G (6½ OUNCES) BUTTER, CHOPPED COARSELY, EXTRA

2 EGGS

1 TABLESPOON PLAIN (ALL-PURPOSE) FLOUR

POACHED PEARS

½ CUP (125ML) LEMON JUICE

½ CUP (175G) HONEY

2 CUPS (500ML) WATER

½ CUP (110G) CASTER (SUPERFINE) SUGAR

1 VANILLA BEAN, SPLIT LENGTHWAYS

6 GREEN PEARS (1.2KG), PEELED, QUARTERED

HONEYED WALNUTS

¾ CUP (75G) WALNUTS

1 TABLESPOON HONEY

1 Process butter, icing sugar, flour and cocoa until mixture resembles breadcrumbs. Add egg yolk and the water; process until ingredients come together. Enclose in plastic wrap; refrigerate for 30 minutes.

2 Roll pastry between sheets of baking paper until 5mm (¼-inch) thick. Freeze 5 minutes. Lift pastry into an 11cm x 35cm (4½-inch x 14-inch) rectangular loose-based fluted tart tin, press into sides, trim edges; prick base all over with a fork. Freeze for 20 minutes.

3 Meanwhile, preheat oven to 200°C/400°F.

4 Place tart tin on an oven tray; line with baking paper, fill with dried beans or rice. Bake for 15 minutes. Remove paper and beans; bake a further 10 minutes or until browned lightly. Cool on tray.

5 Reduce oven to 180°C/350°F.

6 Stir chocolate and extra butter in a heatproof medium bowl over a saucepan of simmering water until just melted. Remove bowl from pan; whisk in egg and flour until just combined. Pour mixture into pastry case; smooth surface.

7 Bake tart for 20 minutes or until just set. Cool. Cover; refrigerate for 3 hours or overnight.

8 Meanwhile, make poached pears, then honeyed walnuts.

9 Stand tart at room temperature for 30 minutes before serving; top with walnuts and syrup, accompanied with pears.

poached pears Heat juice, honey, the water, sugar and vanilla bean in a medium saucepan over a low heat; cook, stirring, until sugar dissolves. Bring to the boil over a high heat; reduce heat to medium-low. Add pears; cook for 20 minutes or until just tender. Remove pears from syrup with a slotted spoon. Return syrup to the boil over high heat. Boil 10 minutes or until thickened slightly.

honeyed walnuts Place walnuts on a baking-paper-lined oven tray. Drizzle with honey; toss to coat. Bake at 180°C/350°F for 12 minutes, stirring halfway, until golden. Cool.

APPLE CINNAMON CRUNCH CAKE WITH ANGLAISE

PREP + COOK TIME **2 HOURS (+ REFRIGERATION & STANDING)** SERVES **8**

8 SMALL RED-SKINNED APPLES (800G) (SEE TIP)

1.5 LITRES (6 CUPS) WATER

2 CUPS (440G) CASTER (SUPERFINE) SUGAR

1 CINNAMON STICK

180G (6 OUNCES) BUTTER, SOFTENED

2 TEASPOONS VANILLA EXTRACT

1 CUP (220G) CASTER (SUPERFINE) SUGAR, EXTRA

3 EGGS

1 CUP (120G) GROUND ALMONDS

1½ CUPS (225G) SELF-RAISING FLOUR

½ CUP (125ML) BUTTERMILK

CINNAMON CRUNCH TOPPING

45G (1½ OUNCES) BUTTER

¼ CUP (55G) BROWN SUGAR

¼ CUP (35G) PLAIN (ALL-PURPOSE) FLOUR

1½ TEASPOONS GROUND CINNAMON

ANGLAISE

¾ CUP (180ML) POURING CREAM

1⅓ CUPS (330ML) MILK

1 CINNAMON STICK

4 EGG YOLKS

¼ CUP (55G) CASTER (SUPERFINE) SUGAR

1 Peel apples, leaving stems intact.

2 Combine the water, sugar and cinnamon in a saucepan large enough to hold apples in a single layer; stir over high heat, without boiling, until sugar dissolves. Bring to the boil, add apples; cover apples with a round of baking paper and a heatproof plate to keep apples submerged in syrup. Return to the boil. Reduce heat; simmer, covered, for 8 minutes or until apples are tender. Remove apples from pan with a slotted spoon. Cool for 10 minutes.

3 Preheat oven to 160°C/325°F. Insert base of a 26cm (10½-inch) springform pan upside down in pan to make cake easier to remove. Grease closed pan. Line base with baking paper.

4 Beat butter, extract and extra sugar in a small bowl with an electric mixer until light and fluffy. Beat in eggs, one at a time. Transfer mixture to a large bowl. Stir in ground almonds, sifted flour and buttermilk, in two batches. Spread mixture into pan.

5 Place apples, evenly spaced, around outside edge of pan, pushing apples down to the base of pan. Bake cake for 30 minutes.

6 Meanwhile, make cinnamon crunch topping.

7 Crumble topping over cake; bake for a further 45 minutes. Stand cake in pan for 15 minutes.

8 Meanwhile, make anglaise; serve with warm cake.

cinnamon crunch topping Melt butter in a small saucepan; stir in remaining ingredients. Refrigerate for 15 minutes.

anglaise Bring cream, milk and cinnamon to the boil in a medium saucepan. Remove from heat, cover; stand for 20 minutes. Whisk egg yolks and sugar in a medium bowl until creamy. Gradually whisk in warm milk mixture. Return to pan; stir over medium-high heat, without boiling, until mixture thickens and coats the back of a spoon. Strain into a medium jug; discard cinnamon stick.

tip *We used very small pink lady apples.*

TIRAMISU PUDDING WITH MASCARPONE CREAM

PREP + COOK TIME **1 HOUR** SERVES **8**

1 CUP (150G) SELF-RAISING FLOUR
2 TABLESPOONS DUTCH-PROCESSED COCOA
½ CUP (110G) CASTER (SUPERFINE) SUGAR
½ CUP (125ML) MILK
1 EGG, BEATEN LIGHTLY
2 TABLESPOONS GOLDEN SYRUP
150G (4½ OUNCES) BUTTER, MELTED, COOLED
1 CUP (220G) FIRMLY PACKED BROWN SUGAR
1 TABLESPOON INSTANT ESPRESSO COFFEE GRANULES
1 CUP (250ML) BOILING WATER
¼ CUP (60ML) MARSALA
½ CUP (125ML) THICKENED (HEAVY) CREAM
2 TEASPOONS DUTCH-PROCESSED COCOA, EXTRA

MASCARPONE CREAM
250G (8 OUNCES) MASCARPONE CHEESE
¾ CUP (180ML) THICKENED (HEAVY) CREAM
2 TABLESPOONS ICING (CONFECTIONERS') SUGAR

1 Preheat oven to 180°C/350°F. Grease a 1.5-litre (6-cup) shallow ovenproof dish.
2 Sift flour and cocoa into a large bowl; stir in caster sugar, milk, egg, syrup and half the butter. Spread mixture into dish.
3 Stir the brown sugar, coffee granules and the water in a medium heatproof jug until sugar is dissolved. Stir in marsala, cream and remaining butter. Slowly pour coffee mixture over the back of a spoon, over pudding batter.
4 Bake pudding for 40 minutes or until firm in the centre. Stand for 5 minutes.
5 Meanwhile, make mascarpone cream.
6 Dust pudding with extra cocoa; serve with mascarpone cream.

mascarpone cream Beat mascarpone, cream and sifted icing sugar in a small bowl with an electric mixer until soft peaks form.

tip This pudding is best made close to serving as the sauce will thicken and be absorbed if left to stand.

TANGELO TART WITH CANDIED BLOOD ORANGES

PREP + COOK TIME **1 HOURS 50 MINUTES (+ REFRIGERATION & COOLING)**
SERVES **8**

1½ CUPS (225G) PLAIN (ALL-PURPOSE) FLOUR

2 TABLESPOONS ICING (CONFECTIONERS') SUGAR

125G (4 OUNCES) COLD BUTTER, CHOPPED

1 EGG YOLK

1 TABLESPOON CHILLED WATER

1 TABLESPOON FINELY GRATED TANGELO RIND

½ CUP (125ML) STRAINED FRESHLY SQUEEZED TANGELO JUICE

5 EGGS

¾ CUP (165G) CASTER (SUPERFINE) SUGAR

300ML POURING CREAM

CANDIED BLOOD ORANGES

½ CUP (110G) CASTER (SUPERFINE) SUGAR

1½ CUPS (375ML) WATER

½ CUP (125ML) STRAINED FRESHLY SQUEEZED BLOOD ORANGE JUICE

3 MEDIUM BLOOD ORANGES (480G), CUT INTO 5MM (¼-INCH) SLICES

½ CUP (180G) HONEY

1 Process flour, sugar and butter until mixture resembles breadcrumbs. Add egg yolk and the water; process until ingredients just come together. Wrap pastry in plastic wrap; refrigerate for 30 minutes.

2 Grease a 3cm (1¼-inch) deep, 23cm (9¼-inch) round loose-based tart tin. Roll pastry between sheets of baking paper until 3mm (⅛-inch) thick and large enough to line the tin. Lift pastry into tin, ease into base and side, trim edge; prick base all over with a fork. Cover; refrigerate for 20 minutes.

3 Meanwhile, preheat oven to 190°C/375°F.

4 Place tin on an oven tray; line pastry with baking paper, fill with dried beans or rice. Bake for 10 minutes. Remove paper and beans; bake a further 10 minutes or until browned lightly. Cool on tray.

5 Reduce oven to 170°C/325°F.

6 Whisk rind, juice, eggs, caster sugar and cream in a large bowl until combined. Strain mixture into pastry case.

7 Bake tart for 35 minutes or until just set. Cool. Cover; refrigerate for 3 hours or overnight.

8 Make candied blood oranges.

9 Stand tart at room temperature for 30 minutes before serving; top with half the candied oranges and a little syrup. Serve tart cut into slices with remaining candied oranges and syrup.

candied blood oranges Stir sugar, water and juice in a large frying pan over medium heat until sugar dissolves. Add orange slices; simmer, for 20 minutes or until rind is soft. Add honey to pan; simmer a further 15 minutes or until oranges are candied and syrup is thickened.

tip *The tart can be made a day ahead. The candied blood oranges are best made close to serving.*

SPICED PUMPKIN
& HONEY PIES

PREP + COOK TIME 1¾ HOURS (+ REFRIGERATION & COOLING)
MAKES 6

1½ CUPS (225G) PLAIN (ALL-PURPOSE) FLOUR
125G (4 OUNCES) COLD BUTTER, CHOPPED
2 TABLESPOONS ICING (CONFECTIONERS') SUGAR
1 EGG YOLK
1 TABLESPOON CHILLED WATER
1 EGG YOLK, EXTRA
½ CUP (125ML) THICK (DOUBLE) CREAM
3 TEASPOONS HONEY
¼ CUP (25G) COARSELY CHOPPED WALNUTS

SPICED PUMPKIN FILLING
1KG (2 POUNDS) JAP OR BUTTERNUT PUMPKIN, CHOPPED COARSELY
PINCH OF SEA SALT
¾ TEASPOON GROUND GINGER
½ TEASPOON GROUND CINNAMON
2 EGGS
2 TABLESPOONS MILK
¼ CUP (90G) HONEY
2 TABLESPOONS CASTER (SUPERFINE) SUGAR

1 Process flour, butter and sugar until mixture resembles breadcrumbs. Add egg yolk and the water; process until ingredients come together. Divide pastry into six portions, wrap each in plastic wrap; refrigerate for 30 minutes.

2 Meanwhile, make spiced pumpkin filling.

3 Roll pastry between sheets of baking paper until large enough to line six 10cm (4-inch) round, 3cm (1¼-inch) deep, loose-based tart tins. Lift pastry into tins, press into base and sides, trim the edge; prick bases all over with a fork. Cover; refrigerate for 20 minutes.

4 Meanwhile, preheat oven to 180°C/350°F.

5 Place tins on an oven tray; line each with baking paper, fill with dried beans or rice. Bake for 15 minutes. Remove paper and beans; bake for a further 10 minutes or until browned lightly. Cool on tray.

6 Spoon pumpkin filling into pastry cases. Brush tops with extra egg yolk. Bake pies for 25 minutes or until set and light golden.

7 Just before serving, spoon cream onto pies, drizzle with honey and top with nuts.

spiced pumpkin filling Boil, steam or microwave pumpkin until just tender; drain. Process pumpkin, salt, ginger and cinnamon until smooth. Add eggs, milk, honey and sugar; process until smooth. Cool.

tip *The pies can be made a day ahead. Before serving, reheat in a 160°C/325°F oven for 10 minutes or until warm.*

RHUBARB &
CUSTARD BREAD
PUDDING

PREP + COOK TIME **1½ HOURS (+ COOLING & STANDING)** SERVES **8**

1¾ CUPS (430ML) POURING
  CREAM
1½ CUPS (375ML) MILK
1 VANILLA BEAN,
  SPLIT LENGTHWAYS
700G (1½-POUND) LOAF
  SLICED WHITE BREAD,
  CRUSTS REMOVED
60G (2 OUNCES) BUTTER,
  SOFTENED
6 EGGS
¾ CUP (165G) CASTER
  (SUPERFINE) SUGAR
20G (¾ OUNCE) BUTTER,
  MELTED, EXTRA
2 TABLESPOONS DEMERARA
  SUGAR

RHUBARB & RASPBERRY JAM
700G (1½ POUNDS)
  TRIMMED RHUBARB,
  CHOPPED COARSELY
½ CUP (110G) CASTER
  (SUPERFINE) SUGAR
⅓ CUP (80ML) WATER
⅔ CUP (100G) FROZEN
  RASPBERRIES

1 Make rhubarb and raspberry jam.

2 Preheat oven to 160°C/325°F. Grease a 2-litre (8-cup) baking dish.

3 Place cream, milk and vanilla bean in a medium saucepan over medium heat. Bring to a simmer; stand for 15 minutes.

4 Meanwhile, spread bread slices with butter. Spread slices with tablespoons of jam. Roll slices to enclose filling. Halve slices crossways. Arrange bread, cut-side up, in dish.

5 Whisk eggs and caster sugar in a large bowl until combined; whisk in cream mixture. Strain custard mixture over bread; stand for 15 minutes.

6 Brush top of pudding with extra butter; sprinkle with demerara sugar.

7 Bake pudding for 40 minutes or until just set. Stand pudding for 10 minutes before serving.

rhubarb & raspberry jam Place ingredients in a large saucepan over medium heat; bring to a simmer. Simmer, uncovered, for 15 minutes or until thick; cool.

tips *You will need about 1 large bunch rhubarb for this recipe.*

To test if pudding is cooked, insert a small sharp knife into the centre then withdraw the blade. If the blade is clean, the pudding is ready.

PISTACHIO, WALNUT & CHOCOLATE BAKLAVA

PREP + COOK TIME **1 HOUR 10 MINUTES (+ COOLING & STANDING)**
MAKES **36**

12 SHEETS FILLO PASTRY
120G (4 OUNCES) BUTTER, MELTED
2 TABLESPOONS FINELY CHOPPED WALNUTS

FILLING
1½ CUPS (210G) PISTACHIOS
2 CUPS (200G) WALNUTS
200G (6 OUNCES) DARK (SEMI-SWEET) CHOCOLATE, CHOPPED COARSELY
⅓ CUP (75G) CASTER (SUPERFINE) SUGAR
2 TEASPOONS GROUND CINNAMON
1½ TABLESPOONS FINELY GRATED ORANGE RIND

HONEY SYRUP
1½ CUPS (330G) CASTER (SUPERFINE) SUGAR
1½ CUPS (375ML) WATER
½ CUP (175G) HONEY
1 MEDIUM ORANGE (240G), RIND PEELED IN LONG STRIPS
⅓ CUP (80ML) ORANGE JUICE

1 Preheat oven to 190°C/375°F. Grease a 22cm x 40cm x 2.5cm (9-inch x 16-inch x 1-inch) oven tray, then line with baking paper.
2 Make filling.
3 Layer three pastry sheets, brushing each with a little of the butter. Spread a quarter of the filling over pastry, leaving a 3cm (1¼-inch) border along both long sides. Starting at one long side, roll up pastry to form a log. Place log on oven tray, brush with butter. Repeat with remaining pastry, butter and filling.
4 Bake baklava for 20 minutes or until golden.
5 Meanwhile, make honey syrup.
6 Stand baklava on tray for 5 minutes to cool slightly. Using a small sharp knife, cut each log, on the diagonal, into nine 2cm (¾-inch) wide pieces in the tray. Pour hot syrup over baklava; stand for 3 hours or until syrup is absorbed. Serve topped with chopped walnuts.

filling Place nuts on an oven tray; roast in oven for 5 minutes or until browned lightly. Cool completely. Process nuts with remaining ingredients until finely chopped.

honey syrup Stir sugar, the water, honey and rind in a small saucepan, over medium heat, without boiling, until sugar dissolves. Bring to a simmer. Simmer for 20 minutes or until thickened slightly. Stir in juice.

serving suggestion Serve with greek-style yoghurt.

RICOTTA & CHOCOLATE CHEESECAKE WITH GRAPES

PREP + COOK TIME **1½ HOURS (+ COOLING & REFRIGERATION)**
SERVES **12**

1 VANILLA BEAN

750G (1½ POUNDS) RICOTTA

½ CUP (175G) HONEY

2 TABLESPOONS CASTER (SUPERFINE) SUGAR

2 TEASPOONS FINELY GRATED ORANGE RIND

3 FREE-RANGE EGGS

150G (4½ OUNCES) DARK CHOCOLATE (70% COCOA), CHOPPED FINELY

1½ CUPS (240G) RED AND BLACK GRAPES

1 TABLESPOON HONEY, EXTRA

1 Preheat oven to 150°C/300°F. Grease a 22cm (9-inch) springform pan; line base and side with baking paper, extending the paper 3cm (1¼ inches) above the edge.

2 Split vanilla bean in half lengthways; scrape seeds into a large bowl of an electric mixer. Add ricotta, honey, sugar and rind; beat with an electric mixer on medium-high speed for 3 minutes or until smooth. Beat in eggs, one at time, until just combined. Stir in chocolate and one-third of the red and black grapes. Pour mixture into pan.

3 Bake cheesecake for 55 minutes or until the centre is almost firm to touch. Turn oven off; cool in oven with door ajar. Refrigerate cheesecake for 4 hours or until firm.

4 Just before serving, cut some of the remaining red grapes in half; top cheesecake with all remaining grapes. Drizzle with extra honey.

tips When chopping the chocolate aim for fairly even pieces about 5mm (¼-inch) in size.

Cooling the cheesecake in the oven after it has been turned off, ensures that it will cool slowly and prevent the top from cracking.

RUSTIC APPLE PIE

PREP + COOK TIME **1 HOUR 20 MINUTES (+ REFRIGERATION)** SERVES **8**

4 MEDIUM RED-SKINNED APPLES (600G)
1 CUP (220G) CASTER (SUPERFINE) SUGAR
2 TEASPOONS FINELY GRATED LEMON RIND
1 TABLESPOON LEMON JUICE
3 CUPS (750ML) WATER
2 CUPS (300G) PLAIN (ALL-PURPOSE) FLOUR
1 TABLESPOON CASTER (SUPERFINE) SUGAR, EXTRA
125G (4 OUNCES) COLD UNSALTED BUTTER, CHOPPED
⅓ CUP (80ML) ICED WATER, APPROXIMATELY
2 TABLESPOONS MILK
3 TABLESPOONS DEMERARA SUGAR
1 TABLESPOON FLAKED NATURAL ALMONDS

1 Peel and core apples; cut into sixths. Place apple in a medium saucepan with caster sugar, rind, juice and the water. Bring to the boil. Reduce heat to low; simmer for 10 minutes or until tender. Using a slotted spoon, transfer apple to a medium bowl. Simmer syrup, uncovered, for 15 minutes or until reduced to ¾ cup. Cool.

2 Meanwhile, process flour, extra sugar and butter until crumbly. Add enough of the iced water to process until ingredients come together. Press dough into a ball, enclose in plastic wrap; refrigerate for 30 minutes.

3 Preheat oven to 180°C/350°F.

4 Roll dough between two large sheets of baking paper into a 35cm (14-inch) round. Remove top layer of paper; carefully slide dough on paper onto a large oven tray.

5 Pile apple into the centre of the dough, leaving a 7cm (2¾-inch) border. Fold pastry edge up and around apple. Brush milk over pastry; sprinkle with demerara sugar.

6 Bake pie for 40 minutes or until the pastry is golden brown. Just before serving, spoon some of the syrup over the pie; sprinkle with almonds.

tips *If you would like to give the pie some colour, add a scatter of frozen raspberries or blueberries to the apples before wrapping in the pastry.*

The pie can be made 6 hours ahead. Reheat 20 minutes before serving.

serving suggestion
Serve with cream, ice-cream or custard.

BANANA COFFEE CAKE WITH SALTED CARAMEL FROSTING

PREP + COOK TIME 3 HOURS (+ REFRIGERATION) SERVES 12

395G (12½ OUNCES) CANNED SWEETENED CONDENSED MILK

300G (9½ OUNCES) BUTTER, SOFTENED, CHOPPED

¾ CUP (165G) FIRMLY PACKED BROWN SUGAR

2 EGGS

1½ CUPS (225G) SELF-RAISING FLOUR

½ TEASPOON BICARBONATE OF SODA (BAKING SODA)

1 TEASPOON GROUND CINNAMON

1½ CUPS (360G) MASHED RIPE BANANA (SEE TIP)

½ CUP (120G) SOUR CREAM

1 CUP (100G) WALNUT HALVES, ROASTED, CHOPPED

3 TEASPOONS INSTANT ESPRESSO COFFEE GRANULES

¼ CUP (60ML) BOILING WATER

1 TEASPOON SEA SALT FLAKES

1 Preheat oven to 220°C/425°F. Grease a deep 20cm (8-inch) round cake pan; line base with baking paper.

2 Pour condensed milk into a 2-litre (8-cup) ceramic ovenproof dish. Cover dish with foil; crush excess foil upwards. Place ceramic dish in a larger baking dish; add enough boiling water into the baking dish to come halfway up side of the ceramic dish. Bake for 1 hour. Stir mixture; cover, bake for a further 30 minutes or until mixture is a golden caramel colour, adding extra boiling water to baking dish as needed to maintain water level during baking. Remove ceramic dish from water. Whisk in 170g (5½ ounces) of the butter, piece by piece, until melted and caramel is smooth. Cover; refrigerate for 1 hour, stirring occasionally until mixture is cold and firm.

3 Reduce oven to 180°C/350°F.

4 Beat remaining butter and the sugar in a small bowl with an electric mixer until pale and fluffy. Beat in eggs, one at a time, until just combined. Transfer mixture to a large bowl. Stir in sifted dry ingredients with mashed banana, sour cream, nuts and combined coffee and water. Spread mixture in pan.

5 Bake cake for 1 hour or until a skewer inserted into the centre comes out clean. Stand cake in pan for 5 minutes before turning, top-side up, onto a wire rack to cool.

6 Beat cold caramel mixture in a small bowl with an electric mixer for 1 minute or until paler and fluffy. Spread caramel frosting on top of cooled cake. Just before serving, sprinkle with salt.

tip *You will need about 4 medium bananas for the amount of mashed banana required.*

MANDARIN ALMOND CAKES WITH CANDIED CUMQUATS

PREP + COOK TIME **1 HOUR (+ COOLING)** MAKES **8**

1¼ CUPS (185G) SELF-RAISING FLOUR

½ TEASPOON BICARBONATE OF SODA (BAKING SODA)

1 CUP (120G) GROUND ALMONDS

1¼ CUPS (275G) CASTER (SUPERFINE) SUGAR

½ CUP (125ML) EXTRA VIRGIN OLIVE OIL

1 TABLESPOON FINELY GRATED MANDARIN RIND

½ CUP (125ML) STRAINED FRESHLY SQUEEZED MANDARIN JUICE

3 EGGS, BEATEN LIGHTLY

1¼ CUPS (290G) FRESH RICOTTA

½ CUP (80G) ICING (CONFECTIONERS') SUGAR

⅔ CUP (160ML) THICK (DOUBLE) CREAM (51% FAT)

CANDIED CUMQUATS

325G (10½ OUNCES) CUMQUATS, HALVED, SEEDS REMOVED

1 CUP (220G) CASTER (SUPERFINE) SUGAR

¾ CUP (180ML) WATER

2 TABLESPOONS LIME JUICE

1 Make candied cumquats

2 Preheat oven to 180°C/350°F. Grease eight 10cm (4-inch) springform pans. Line bases and sides with baking paper.

3 Sift flour, soda and ground almonds into a large bowl, pushing mixture through with a wooden spoon. Stir in caster sugar. Whisk oil, rind, juice and eggs in a small bowl; add to dry ingredients, whisk until mixture is smooth. Spoon mixture into pans.

4 Bake cakes for 25 minutes or until a skewer inserted into the centre comes out clean. Stand in tins until cooled.

5 Meanwhile, process ricotta and sifted icing sugar until smooth; transfer to a medium bowl. Gently fold in cream until combined.

6 Serve cakes topped with ricotta cream and candied cumquats.

candied cumquats Place cumquats in a small saucepan of water; bring to the boil. Drain. Repeat process (this is to help remove any bitterness and soften the rind). Stir sugar and the water in a small saucepan over low heat until sugar dissolves. Increase heat to high; bring to the boil. Add cumquats; simmer for 30 minutes or until soft and translucent, and syrup is reduced. Cool. Stir in juice.

MAPLE BAKED
WINTER FRUITS

PREP + COOK TIME **45 MINUTES** SERVES **6**

1 MEDIUM ORANGE (240G)

1 CUP (250ML) DRY WHITE WINE

3 SMALL RED APPLES (400G)

3 CORELLA PEARS (405G)

30G (1 OUNCE) UNSALTED BUTTER, SOFTENED

½ CUP (125ML) PURE MAPLE SYRUP

450G (14½ OUNCES) RHUBARB, TRIMMED, CUT INTO 12CM (4¾-INCHES) LENGTHS

250G (8 OUNCES) MASCARPONE OR CRÈME FRAÎCHE

1 Preheat oven to 180°C/350°F.

2 Using a vegetable peeler, peel rind from orange in one long strip, if possible. Squeeze juice from orange. Place juice, rind and wine in a large shallow baking dish.

3 Halve apples crossways; trim the bases slightly to give them a flat surface to sit on. Halve the pears lengthways; trim the rounded skin sides slightly, to give them a flat surface to sit on. Place apples and pears in baking dish, trimmed-side down.

4 Rub softened butter generously over apples and pears; drizzle with maple syrup. Cover dish with foil; bake for 20 minutes. Add rhubarb; bake, covered, for a further 10 minutes. Remove foil; bake for a further 5 minutes or until all fruit are tender.

5 Combine mascarpone with 2 tablespoons of the cooking liquid from the baked fruit.

6 Serve baked fruit with mascarpone.

serving suggestion
Serve with almond biscotti or shortbread.

PEAR & GINGER
UPSIDE-DOWN
CAKE

PREP + COOK TIME **1 HOUR 20 MINUTES** SERVES **8**

3 MEDIUM PEARS (630G)

1½ CUPS (330G) FIRMLY PACKED BROWN SUGAR

1 CUP (250ML) VEGETABLE OIL

1 MEDIUM ORANGE (240G), RIND FINELY GRATED

2 TEASPOONS FINELY GRATED FRESH GINGER

3 EGGS

2½ CUPS (375G) PLAIN (ALL-PURPOSE) FLOUR

2½ TEASPOONS BAKING POWDER

½ CUP (125ML) MILK

ORANGE CINNAMON SYRUP

⅓ CUP (80ML) FRESHLY SQUEEZED STRAINED ORANGE JUICE

60G (2 OUNCES) BUTTER

1 CUP (220G) FIRMLY PACKED BROWN SUGAR

½ TEASPOON GROUND CINNAMON

1 Preheat oven to 220°C/425°F. Grease and line a 24cm (9½ inch) round cake pan.

2 Make orange cinnamon syrup.

3 Peel and core pears; cut each into eight wedges. Arrange pear in a decorative pattern on base of cake pan; pour syrup over pears.

4 Beat sugar, oil, rind, ginger and eggs in a large bowl with an electric mixer until combined. Gently add combined sifted flour and baking powder, then milk. Carefully pour batter over pears.

5 Bake cake for 10 minutes. Reduce heat to 180°C/350°F; bake for a further 55 minutes or until a skewer inserted into the centre of the cake comes out clean. Cool cake completely in the pan before carefully turning out onto a platter.

orange cinnamon syrup
Place ingredients in a small saucepan; bring to the boil. Reduce heat; simmer over medium heat for 3 minutes or until thickened slightly. Cool.

serving suggestion
Serve with vanilla ice-cream.

VANILLA & RED
WINE POACHED
PEARS

PREP + COOK TIME **40 MINUTES (+ COOLING & REFRIGERATION)**
SERVES **6**

6 MEDIUM FIRM PEARS (1.4KG)
2 CUPS (500ML) DRY RED WINE
1½ CUPS (375ML) WATER
**2 X 5CM (2-INCH) PIECES
  ORANGE RIND**
½ CUP (125ML) ORANGE JUICE
**1 CUP (220G) CASTER
  (SUPERFINE) SUGAR**
1 VANILLA BEAN
1 CINNAMON STICK

1 Peel pears, leaving stems intact.
2 Combine wine, the water, rind, juice and sugar in a large saucepan. Halve vanilla bean lengthways, scrape seeds into pan; add vanilla bean and cinnamon stick.
3 Lay pears down in pan to cover in wine mixture. Cover surface with a round of baking paper and a heatproof small plate to keep pears submerged. Bring to the boil. Reduce heat; simmer, covered, over medium-low heat for 20 minutes or until pears are tender. Transfer pears to a large deep bowl. Cover to keep warm.
4 Meanwhile, simmer remaining syrup in pan over medium heat, for 10 minutes or until syrupy.
5 Serve warm or cooled pears drizzled with reduced syrup.

tips We used packham pears in this recipe.

Add a squeeze of lemon juice to the reduced syrup if it is too sweet.

serving suggestion
Serve with whipped cream or vanilla ice-cream.

WARM STRAWBERRY RHUBARB CRUMBLES

PREP + COOK TIME **50 MINUTES** SERVES **6**

500G (1 POUND) RHUBARB

250G (8 OUNCES) STRAWBERRIES

¼ CUP (55G) CASTER (SUPERFINE) SUGAR

2 TEASPOONS VANILLA EXTRACT

2 EGGS

¼ CUP (55G) CASTER (SUPERFINE) SUGAR, EXTRA

1 TABLESPOON CORNFLOUR (CORNSTARCH)

300ML POURING CREAM

1 CUP (250ML) MILK

2 TEASPOONS VANILLA EXTRACT, EXTRA

CRUMBLE

½ CUP (75G) SELF-RAISING FLOUR

¼ CUP (55G) DEMERARA SUGAR

60G (2 OUNCES) COLD BUTTER, CHOPPED FINELY

½ CUP (60G) COARSELY CHOPPED PECANS

1 Preheat oven to 180°C/350°F.

2 Trim rhubarb and chop into 5cm (2-inch) pieces. Hull strawberries. Combine rhubarb, strawberries, sugar and extract in a shallow baking dish. Bake, uncovered, for 20 minutes or until rhubarb softens.

3 Meanwhile, make crumble.

4 Whisk eggs, extra sugar and cornflour in a medium saucepan over medium heat until combined. Gradually whisk in cream and milk; cook, whisking, until mixture boils and thickens. Remove from heat; stir in extra extract.

5 Pour custard into six serving bowls. Top with rhubarb mixture, then crumble.

crumble Line an oven tray with baking paper. Combine sifted flour and sugar in a medium bowl; rub in butter until crumbly, stir in nuts. Spoon mixture in a thin layer onto tray. Bake for 15 minutes or until mixture is browned lightly. Cool for 10 minutes before crumbling mixture coarsely.

RUBY GRAPEFRUIT
MERINGUE PIES

PREP + COOK TIME **1½ HOURS (+ COOLING & REFRIGERATION)**
MAKES **6**

1⅔ CUPS (250G) PLAIN (ALL-PURPOSE) FLOUR

185G (6 OUNCES) COLD BUTTER, CHOPPED

2 TABLESPOONS ICED WATER

RUBY GRAPEFRUIT CURD

5 EGG YOLKS

½ CUP (110G) CASTER (SUPERFINE) SUGAR

150G (5 OUNCES) BUTTER, CHOPPED

2 TEASPOONS FINELY GRATED RUBY RED GRAPEFRUIT RIND

¾ CUP (180ML) FRESH RUBY RED GRAPEFRUIT JUICE

MERINGUE

⅔ CUP (150G) CASTER (SUPERFINE) SUGAR

½ CUP (125ML) WATER

4 EGG WHITES

PINCH CREAM OF TARTAR

1 Make ruby grapefruit curd.

2 Process flour and butter until mixture resembles breadcrumbs. Add the water; process until ingredients just come together. Form into a disc, wrap in plastic wrap; refrigerate for 30 minutes.

3 Grease six 10cm (4-inch) round straight-sided tart tins. Divide pastry into six portions. Roll out each portion on a floured surface or between sheets of baking paper until large enough to line tins. Lift pastry into tins; press into bases and sides, trim excess pastry. Prick bases all over with a fork, place pans on oven tray; refrigerate for 30 minutes.

4 Preheat oven to 200°C/400°F.

5 Line pastry with baking paper; fill with dried beans or rice. Bake for 15 minutes. Remove paper and beans; bake for a further 10 minutes or until browned lightly and crisp. Cool. Spread curd into cases.

6 Make meringue; increase oven to 230°C/460°F.

7 Spoon meringue into a piping bag fitted with a 1.5cm (¾-inch) plain tube; pipe meringue onto pies. Just before serving, place pies in oven for 2 minutes until browned. Serve immediately.

ruby grapefruit curd Whisk egg yolks and sugar in a medium heatproof bowl over a medium saucepan of simmering water. Add butter, rind and juice; cook, stirring, until mixture coats the back of a spoon. Pour into a clean medium heatproof bowl, cover surface with plastic wrap; refrigerate until cool.

meringue Stir sugar and the water in a small saucepan over high heat, without boiling, until sugar dissolves. Bring to the boil. Reduce heat; simmer, uncovered, without stirring, until syrup reaches 115°C/240°F on a candy thermometer. When syrup reaches 115°C, start beating egg whites and cream of tartar in a medium bowl with an electric mixer until soft peaks form. While beating egg whites, bring sugar syrup to 121°C/250°F. With motor operating, gradually pour syrup into egg white in a thin steady stream; continue beating until mixture is thick, glossy and cooled to room temperature.

PEANUT BUTTER
CHOCOLATE CAKE

PREP + COOK TIME 1½ HOURS (+ REFRIGERATION) SERVES 12

½ CUP (50G) DUTCH-
  PROCESSED COCOA

½ CUP (125ML) BOILING WATER

185G (6 OUNCES) BUTTER,
  SOFTENED

1½ CUPS (330G) CASTER
  (SUPERFINE) SUGAR

1 TEASPOON VANILLA
  EXTRACT

3 EGGS

¼ CUP (70G) SMOOTH
  PEANUT BUTTER

1½ CUPS (225G)
  SELF-RAISING FLOUR

½ CUP (75G) PLAIN
  (ALL-PURPOSE) FLOUR

¾ CUP (180ML) BUTTERMILK

220G (7 OUNCES) PEANUT-
  BUTTER-FILLED MILK
  CHOCOLATE (33% COCOA),
  CHOPPED COARSELY

PEANUT BUTTER GANACHE

360G (11½ OUNCES) WHITE
  CHOCOLATE, CHOPPED

2 TABLESPOONS SMOOTH
  PEANUT BUTTER

½ CUP (125ML) POURING
  CREAM

1 Preheat oven to 180°C/350°F. Grease a deep 20cm (8-inch) square cake pan; line base and sides with baking paper.

2 Stir cocoa and the water in a small heatproof jug until cocoa dissolves. Cool for 10 minutes.

3 Beat butter, sugar and extract in a small bowl with an electric mixer until pale and fluffy. Beat in eggs, one at a time, then cocoa mixture and peanut butter until combined (mixture may look curdled at this stage). Beat in sifted dry ingredients and buttermilk, in two batches, until smooth. Spread mixture into pan.

4 Bake cake for 1¼ hours or until a skewer inserted into the centre comes out clean. Stand cake in pan for 5 minutes before turning, top-side up, onto a wire rack to cool.

5 Meanwhile, make peanut butter ganache.

6 Beat cold peanut butter ganache with an electric mixer until pale and fluffy. Spread ganache on top of cooled cake; top with peanut-butter-filled chocolate.

peanut butter ganache Place chocolate and peanut butter in a medium heatproof bowl. Heat cream in a small saucepan until almost boiling; pour over chocolate mixture, whisking until smooth. Cover; refrigerate for 1 hour, stirring occasionally until mixture is chilled and thickened.

tip The cake can be made up to 3 days ahead; store in an airtight container at room temperature. The peanut butter ganache is best made on the day of serving.

FLOURLESS CHOCOLATE BEETROOT CAKE

PREP + COOK TIME 2 HOURS (+ REFRIGERATION & COOLING) SERVES 12

300G (9½ OUNCES) BEETROOT (BEETS), PEELED, CUT IN 3CM (1¼-INCH) PIECES

350G (11 OUNCES) DARK CHOCOLATE (70% COCOA), CHOPPED

185G (6 OUNCES) BUTTER, CHOPPED

6 EGGS

1 TEASPOON VANILLA EXTRACT

1 CUP (220G) FIRMLY PACKED BROWN SUGAR

1 CUP (100G) GROUND HAZELNUTS

1 TEASPOON DUTCH-PROCESSED COCOA

CANDIED BEETROOT

1½ CUPS (330G) CASTER (SUPERFINE) SUGAR

1 CUP (250ML) WATER

2 SMALL BEETROOT (BEETS) (200G), PEELED, SLICED THINLY

1 TABLESPOON LEMON JUICE

SWEETENED CRÈME FRAÎCHE

1½ CUPS (360G) CRÈME FRAÎCHE

2 TABLESPOONS ICING (CONFECTIONERS') SUGAR, SIFTED

1 TEASPOON VANILLA EXTRACT

1 Cook beetroot in a small saucepan of boiling water for 45 minutes or until tender. Drain, reserving 2 tablespoons of the cooking liquid. Process beetroot and reserved liquid until smooth. You should have 1 cup beetroot puree.

2 Preheat oven to 160°C/325°F. Grease a 22cm (9-inch) springform pan; line base and side with baking paper.

3 Stir chocolate and butter in a small saucepan over low heat until melted and smooth.

4 Whisk eggs, extract, sugar and ground hazelnuts in a large bowl until combined. Add chocolate mixture and beetroot puree; whisk to combine. Pour mixture into pan; cover with foil.

5 Bake cake for 1 hour 10 minutes or until cooked around the edge with a slight wobble in the centre. Lift up edge of foil to release steam. Refrigerate cake for at least 3 hours or overnight.

6 Make candied beetroot, then sweetened crème fraîche.

7 Place cake on a platter; dust cake edges with cocoa. Spread top of cake with sweetened crème fraîche. Top with candied beetroot and drizzle with reserved syrup.

candied beetroot Stir sugar and the water in a small saucepan over medium heat until sugar dissolves. Bring to the boil. Add beetroot; cook for 20 minutes or until beetroot slices become slightly translucent and syrup thickens. Using two forks, transfer beetroot from syrup to a baking-paper-lined oven tray to cool. Reserve 1 cup of the syrup; stir in juice.

sweetened crème fraîche Whisk ingredients together in a small bowl until soft peaks form.

tip The cake and candied beetroot can be made a day ahead. Store separately in airtight containers in the refrigerator.

PIÑA COLADA CAKE WITH CARAMEL GLAZE

PREP + COOK TIME 1½ HOURS (+ STANDING) SERVES 12

200G (6½ OUNCES) SALTED BUTTER, SOFTENED

¾ CUP (165G) CASTER (SUPERFINE) SUGAR

2 TABLESPOONS COCONUT-FLAVOURED LIQUEUR

3 EGGS

440G (14 OUNCES) CANNED CRUSHED PINEAPPLE IN NATURAL JUICE, DRAINED WELL

⅔ CUP (160ML) COCONUT CREAM

1⅓ CUPS (105G) DESICCATED COCONUT, TOASTED

1¼ CUPS (185G) SELF-RAISING FLOUR

1 TEASPOON BAKING POWDER

CARAMEL GLAZE

1½ CUPS (375ML) THICKENED (HEAVY) CREAM

¾ CUP (165G) FIRMLY PACKED BROWN SUGAR

1½ TABLESPOONS LIQUID GLUCOSE SYRUP (LIGHT CORN SYRUP)

½ TEASPOON SEA SALT FLAKES

1½ TEASPOONS VANILLA EXTRACT

1 Preheat oven to 170°C/340°F. Grease a deep 20cm (8-inch) square cake pan; line base and sides with baking paper.

2 Beat butter, sugar and liqueur in a large bowl with an electric mixer until pale and creamy. Beat in eggs, one at a time, until just combined. Fold in pineapple, coconut cream, desiccated coconut and combined sifted flour and baking powder. Spread mixture into pan.

3 Bake cake for 50 minutes or until a skewer inserted into the centre comes out clean. Stand cake in pan for 15 minutes before turning, top-side up, onto a wire rack to cool.

4 Make caramel glaze.

5 Place cake on a wire rack over an oven tray. Pour two-thirds of the glaze over the cake. Stand for 30 minutes or until glaze is cool and set. Serve cake with remaining glaze.

caramel glaze Bring cream, sugar, glucose and salt to the boil in small saucepan over low heat, stirring until sugar dissolves. Boil for 20 minutes or until caramel is thick and golden. Remove from heat; stir in extract. Cool for 20 minutes or until thickened.

tips *If the remaining caramel glaze thickens too much by the time of serving, reheat in a small saucepan over low heat, adding 1-2 tablespoons extra cream or water to thin it down.*

The cake can be made a day ahead; store in an airtight container at room temperature. The caramel glaze is best made close to serving.

WHOLE ORANGE SEMOLINA CAKE WITH ROSEMARY SYRUP

PREP + COOK TIME **2 HOURS 40 MINUTES (+ STANDING)** SERVES **12**

2 LARGE ORANGES (600G)
1 TEASPOON BAKING POWDER
6 EGGS
1 CUP (220G) CASTER (SUPERFINE) SUGAR
1 CUP (150G) FINE SEMOLINA
1¼ CUPS (150G) GROUND ALMONDS
1½ TEASPOONS FINELY CHOPPED FRESH ROSEMARY LEAVES

ROSEMARY SYRUP
2 LARGE ORANGES (600G)
½ CUP (110G) CASTER (SUPERFINE) SUGAR
½ CUP (125ML) WATER
1½ TABLESPOONS LEMON JUICE
2 TABLESPOONS ORANGE-FLAVOURED LIQUEUR
2 X 8CM (3¼-INCH) SPRIGS FRESH ROSEMARY

1 Place unpeeled oranges in a medium saucepan over high heat, cover with cold water; bring to the boil. Boil, covered, for 1½ hours or until oranges are tender; drain. Cool.

2 Preheat oven to 180°C/350°F. Grease a deep 22cm (9-inch) round cake pan; line base and side with baking paper.

3 Trim and discard ends from oranges. Halve oranges; discard seeds. Process orange, including rind, with baking powder until mixture is pulpy. Transfer to a large bowl.

4 Process eggs and sugar for 5 minutes or until thick and creamy. Stir egg mixture into orange mixture. Fold in semolina, ground almonds and rosemary. Spread mixture into pan.

5 Bake cake for 1 hour or until a skewer inserted into the centre comes out clean. Stand cake in pan for 45 minutes before turning, top-side up, onto a cake plate.

6 Meanwhile, make rosemary syrup.

7 Spoon hot syrup over warm cake. Serve cake warm or at room temperature.

rosemary syrup Remove rind from 1 orange with a zester, into thin strips. Using a vegetable peeler, peel a long continuous strip of rind from remaining orange. Place sugar, the water and juice in a small saucepan over low heat; stir, without boiling, until sugar dissolves. Add long strip of rind, bring to the boil; boil for 5 minutes or until syrup thickens. Remove from heat; stir in liqueur, rosemary and thin strips of rind.

tips If you don't have a zester, simply peel the rind into wide strips with a vegetable peeler, then cut them into thin strips.

The cake is best made on the day of serving.

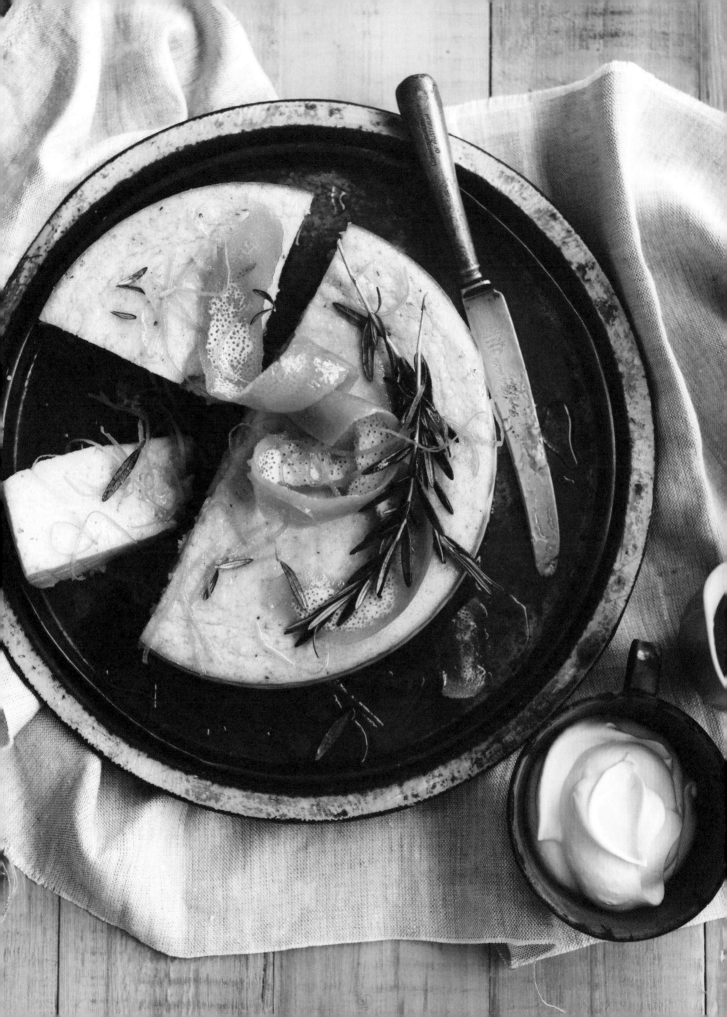

La Mode à tout prix 1943

SPICED SPONGE & RHUBARB ROULADE

PREP + COOK TIME **45 MINUTES (+ COOLING)** SERVES **10**

5 EGGS, SEPARATED

⅔ CUP (150G) CASTER (SUPERFINE) SUGAR

1½ TABLESPOONS HOT WATER

80G (2½ OUNCES) WHITE CHOCOLATE, GRATED FINELY

⅔ CUP (100G) SELF-RAISING FLOUR

1 TEASPOON GROUND CINNAMON

½ TEASPOON GROUND NUTMEG

¼ TEASPOON GROUND CLOVES

¼ TEASPOON GROUND CARDAMOM

¼ CUP (55G) CASTER (SUPERFINE) SUGAR, EXTRA

ROASTED RHUBARB

500G (1 POUND) RHUBARB, TRIMMED, CUT INTO 5CM (2-INCH) LENGTHS

⅓ CUP (75G) FIRMLY PACKED BROWN SUGAR

2 TEASPOONS FINELY GRATED ORANGE RIND

1 TABLESPOON ORANGE JUICE

2.5CM (1-INCH) PIECE FRESH GINGER (12.5G), GRATED

MASCARPONE CREAM

½ CUP (125ML) THICKENED (HEAVY) CREAM

1 CUP (250G) MASCARPONE

1 Preheat oven to 200°C/400°F. Grease a 26cm x 32cm (10½-inch x 12¾-inch) swiss roll pan; line base with baking paper, extending the paper 5cm (2 inches) over the long sides.

2 Beat egg yolks and sugar in a medium bowl with an electric mixer for 5 minutes or until very thick. Pour the hot water down inside of the bowl, add chocolate; gently fold in combined sifted flour and spices until just combined. Transfer to a medium bowl.

3 Beat egg whites in a medium bowl with an electric mixer until soft peaks form. Fold egg whites into chocolate mixture, in two batches, until just combined. Spread mixture into pan.

4 Bake cake for 12 minutes or until golden and sponge springs back when pressed lightly with a finger.

5 Meanwhile, place a piece of baking paper, cut just larger than the pan, on a work surface; sprinkle evenly with extra sugar. Turn hot sponge onto sugar-covered-paper, peel away lining paper; trim crisped edges with a sharp knife.

Working quickly, and using paper as a guide, roll sponge up from a long side. Cool for 5 minutes. Unroll sponge, remove paper; reroll, cover with a clean tea towel. Cool.

6 Meanwhile, make roasted rhubarb. Make mascarpone cream.

7 Unroll sponge; spread with mascarpone cream, leaving a 2.5cm (1-inch) border. Top with rhubarb. Reroll sponge to enclose filling. Serve roulade drizzled with rhubarb pan juices.

roasted rhubarb Combine ingredients in a medium bowl; transfer to a small shallow baking dish. Roast in oven for 10 minutes, stirring halfway, or until rhubarb is tender.

mascarpone cream Beat cream and mascarpone in a small bowl with an electric mixer until soft peaks form.

tip This recipe is best made on the day of serving.

PECAN & SPICED APPLE PULL-APART

PREP + COOK TIME **1 HOUR (+ REFRIGERATION)** SERVES **8**

4 MEDIUM GRANNY SMITH APPLES (600G)

¼ CUP (55G) CASTER (SUPERFINE) SUGAR

1 TABLESPOON BROWN SUGAR

1 TEASPOON GROUND CINNAMON

¼ TEASPOON GROUND CLOVES

1 TABLESPOON WATER

3 CUPS (450G) SELF-RAISING FLOUR

2 TABLESPOONS CASTER (SUPERFINE) SUGAR, EXTRA

40G (1½ OUNCES) COLD BUTTER, CHOPPED

1⅓ CUPS (330ML) BUTTERMILK

½ CUP (60G) PECANS, ROASTED, CHOPPED

1 TABLESPOON BUTTERMILK, EXTRA

CARAMEL SAUCE

1 CUP (220G) FIRMLY PACKED BROWN SUGAR

100G (3 OUNCES) BUTTER, CHOPPED

300ML POURING CREAM

TOPPING

1 TABLESPOON BROWN SUGAR

½ TEASPOON GROUND CINNAMON

¼ CUP (30G) PECANS, ROASTED, CHOPPED

1 Make caramel sauce, then the topping.

2 Preheat oven to 220°C/425°F. Grease a large oven tray; line with baking paper.

3 Peel, core and chop apples into 2cm (¾-inch) pieces. Place apples in a small saucepan with sugars, spices and the water; stir to combine. Bring to a simmer. Reduce heat to low; cook, covered, for 10 minutes or until apples are tender. Cool. Drain apples; discard liquid.

4 Meanwhile, combine flour and extra caster sugar in a large bowl; rub in butter until mixture resembles crumbs. Add buttermilk; using a dinner knife, cut through mixture mixing to a soft dough. Bring dough together gently on a well-floured surface until no longer sticky.

5 Roll out dough on a well-floured piece of baking paper into a 20cm x 40cm (8-inch x 16-inch) rectangle. Position the dough so a long side is in front of you. Spread apple mixture evenly over dough, leaving a 2cm (¾-inch) border on the long side closest to you; scatter with nuts, then drizzle with ¼ cup of the caramel sauce. Using the paper as an aid, roll up dough firmly from the long side; carefully place roll on tray, bringing the two ends together to form a ring. Using a sharp knife, cut eight equally spaced slits into the outside of the ring, towards the centre, cutting three quarters of the way in. Brush scone ring with buttermilk; sprinkle with topping.

6 Bake ring for 20 minutes, cover loosely with foil halfway through cooking to prevent over browning. Serve scone pull-apart warm, drizzled with warmed caramel sauce.

caramel sauce Stir ingredients in a small saucepan over medium heat until sugar dissolves. Simmer for 5 minutes or until thickened slightly.

topping Combine ingredients in a small bowl.

tips *The recipe is best made on day of serving.*

POACHED QUINCE
& CHESTNUT CAKE

PREP + COOK TIME **4 HOURS** SERVES **12**

2 MEDIUM QUINCE (700G), PEELED, QUARTERED, CORED
2 CUPS (440G) CASTER (SUPERFINE) SUGAR
½ CUP (125ML) SWEET MARSALA
2 CINNAMON STICKS, HALVED
1 VANILLA BEAN, SPLIT LENGTHWAYS
1 LITRE (4 CUPS) WATER
1¼ CUPS (185G) SELF-RAISING FLOUR
100G (3 OUNCES) GROUND ALMONDS
½ TEASPOON BAKING POWDER
1 TEASPOON MIXED SPICE
250G (8 OUNCES) BUTTER, SOFTENED
1 CUP (220G) FIRMLY PACKED BROWN SUGAR
1 CUP (220G) UNSWEETENED CHESTNUT PUREE
3 EGGS
¼ CUP (60ML) MILK

CRUMBLE TOPPING
⅓ CUP (50G) PLAIN (ALL-PURPOSE) FLOUR
⅓ CUP (75G) FIRMLY PACKED BROWN SUGAR
⅔ CUP (80G) FINELY CHOPPED WALNUTS
75G (2½ OUNCES) BUTTER, CHOPPED

1 Place quince, caster sugar, marsala, cinnamon, vanilla bean and the water in a large saucepan over high heat; bring to the boil. Reduce heat to low; simmer, uncovered, for 2 hours or until quince is tender and syrup has reduced. Using a slotted spoon, transfer quince into a medium bowl; cool. Reserve syrup and cinnamon. Discard vanilla bean. Cut quince quarters in half.
2 Meanwhile, make crumble topping.
3 Preheat oven to 180°C/350°F. Grease a deep 24cm (9½-inch) springform pan; line base with baking paper.
4 Push flour, ground almonds, baking powder and mixed spice through a fine sieve into a bowl. Beat butter and brown sugar in a large bowl with an electric mixer until paler and fluffy. Add chestnut puree; beat until smooth. Beat in eggs, one at a time, until just combined. Fold in flour mixture and milk until combined. Spread mixture into pan; arrange 12 quince wedges in a circular pattern, then place 4 wedges in the centre. Sprinkle crumble over quince.
5 Bake cake for 1¼ hours or until a skewer inserted into the centre comes out clean. Stand cake in pan for 10 minutes before transferring to a wire rack to cool. Serve warm or cooled, drizzled with reserved syrup and cinnamon.
crumble topping Combine flour, sugar and walnuts in a small bowl. Rub in butter until mixture forms coarse crumbs.

PUMPKIN GINGERBREAD CAKE

PREP + COOK TIME **2¼ HOURS (+ STANDING)** SERVES **12**

- 185G (6 OUNCES) BUTTER, SOFTENED
- 2 TEASPOONS VANILLA EXTRACT
- 5CM (2-INCH) PIECE FRESH GINGER (25G), GRATED FINELY
- 1¼ CUPS (275G) FIRMLY PACKED BROWN SUGAR
- 3 EGGS
- 3 CUPS (450G) SELF-RAISING FLOUR
- 3 TEASPOONS GROUND GINGER
- 1 TEASPOON GROUND CINNAMON
- ½ TEASPOON GROUND NUTMEG
- ¼ TEASPOON GROUND CLOVES
- ¼ TEASPOON COOKING SALT
- ¾ TEASPOON BICARBONATE OF SODA (BAKING SODA)
- 1 CUP (250ML) BUTTERMILK
- 1½ CUPS (350G) MASHED BUTTERNUT PUMPKIN
- 2 TABLESPOONS THINLY SLICED CRYSTALLISED GINGER
- 2 TABLESPOONS COARSELY CHOPPED ROASTED PECANS

CARAMEL SAUCE
- 60G (2 OUNCES) BUTTER
- ½ CUP (110G) FIRMLY PACKED BROWN SUGAR
- 2 TABLESPOONS WATER
- 2 TABLESPOONS DARK RUM

1 Preheat oven to 180°C/350°F. Grease a deep 22cm (9-inch) bundt pan.

2 Beat butter, extract, grated ginger and sugar in a large bowl with an electric mixer until paler and fluffy. Beat in eggs, one at a time, until just combined. Fold in combined sifted flour, ground spices, salt and soda with buttermilk, in two batches, until combined. Stir in pumpkin. Spread mixture into pan; batter should nearly fill the pan.

3 Bake cake on lowest oven shelf for 50 minutes or until a skewer inserted into the centre comes out clean. Stand cake in pan for 15 minutes before turning out onto a wire rack to cool. Level the base of the cake, if necessary.

4 Make caramel sauce.

5 Place cake on a cake stand or plate; drizzle with sauce. Decorate with crystallised ginger and pecans. Serve warm or cold.

caramel sauce Stir butter, sugar and the water in a small saucepan over low heat, without boiling, until butter melts and sugar dissolves. Bring to the boil; boil for 3 minutes or until sauce thickens. Remove from heat; stir in rum. Stand sauce for 5 minutes to thicken.

tips You need to cook 1kg (2 pounds) pumpkin for the amount of mashed pumpkin needed. You can decorate this cake with Chinese candied ginger strips, available from Asian grocers.

The cake and syrup can be made a day ahead; store separately at room temperature.

Glossary

ALLSPICE also known as pimento or jamaican pepper; so-named because it tastes like a combination of nutmeg, cumin, clove and cinnamon. Available whole or ground.

ALMONDS

flaked paper-thin slices.

ground also called almond meal; almonds are powdered to a coarse flour-like texture.

slivered small pieces cut lengthways.

BAHARAT an aromatic spice blend, includes some or all of the following: mixed spice, black pepper, allspice, dried chilli flakes, paprika, coriander seeds, cinnamon, clove, sumac, nutmeg, cumin seeds and cardamom seeds. It can be found in Middle-Eastern food stores, some delicatessens and specialist food stores.

BASIL

sweet the most common type of basil; used extensively in Italian dishes and one of the main ingredients in pesto.

thai also known as horapa; different from holy basil and sweet basil in both look and taste, with smaller leaves and purplish stems. It has a slight aniseed taste and is one of the identifying flavours of Thai food.

BAY LEAVES aromatic leaves from the bay tree available fresh or dried; adds a strong, slightly peppery flavour.

BEAN SPROUTS tender new growths of assorted beans and seeds germinated for consumption as sprouts.

BEANS

black also known as turtle beans or black kidney beans; an earthy-flavoured dried bean completely different from the better-known chinese black beans (which are fermented soya beans).

kidney medium-sized red bean, slightly floury in texture, yet sweet in flavour.

BEETROOT (BEETS) firm, round root vegetable.

BICARBONATE OF SODA (BAKING SODA) a raising agent.

BREAD

ciabatta in Italian, the word means slipper, the traditional shape of this popular crisp-crusted, open-textured white sourdough bread.

sourdough so-named, not because it's sour in taste, but because it's made by using a small amount of 'starter dough', which contains a yeast culture, mixed into flour and water. Part of the resulting dough is then saved to use as the starter dough next time.

tortilla thin, round unleavened bread; can be made at home or purchased frozen, fresh or vacuum-packed. Two kinds are available, one made from wheat flour and the other from corn.

BROCCOLINI a cross between broccoli and chinese kale; it has long asparagus-like stems with a long loose floret, both are edible. Resembles broccoli but is milder and sweeter in taste.

BUK CHOY also called bok choy, pak choi, chinese white cabbage or chinese chard; has a fresh, mild mustard taste.

BUTTER use salted or unsalted (sweet) butter; 125g (4 ounces) is equal to one stick of butter.

CAPERBERRIES olive-sized fruit formed after the buds of the caper bush have flowered; they are usually sold pickled in a vinegar brine with stalks intact.

CAPERS the grey-green buds of a warm climate (usually Mediterranean) shrub, sold either dried and salted or pickled in a vinegar brine; tiny young ones, called baby capers, are also available both in brine or dried in salt.

CARAWAY SEEDS the small, half-moon-shaped dried seed from a member of the parsley family; adds a sharp anise flavour when used in both sweet and savoury dishes. Used widely, in foods such as rye bread, harissa and the classic Hungarian fresh cheese, liptauer.

CARDAMOM a spice native to India and used extensively in its cuisine; can be purchased in pod, seed or ground form. Has a distinctive aromatic, sweetly rich flavour and is one of the world's most expensive spices.

CAVOLO NERO or tuscan cabbage, a staple in Tuscan country cooking. It has long, narrow, wrinkled leaves and a rich and astringent, mild cabbage flavour. It doesn't lose its volume like silver beet or spinach when cooked, but it does need longer cooking.

CELERIAC (CELERY ROOT) tuberous root with knobbly brown skin, white flesh and a celery-like flavour. Keep peeled celeriac in acidulated water to stop it discolouring.

CHEESE

blue mould-treated cheeses mottled with blue veining. Varieties include firm and crumbly stilton types and mild, creamy brie-like cheeses.

bocconcini walnut-sized, baby mozzarella, a delicate, semi-soft, white cheese traditionally made from buffalo milk. Sold fresh, it spoils rapidly so will only keep, refrigerated in brine, for 1 or 2 days at the most.

fetta Greek in origin; a crumbly textured goat- or sheep-milk cheese having a sharp, salty taste. Ripened and stored in salted whey.

fetta, persian a soft, creamy fetta marinated in a blend of olive oil, garlic, herbs and spices; available from most major supermarkets.

fontina a smooth, firm Italian cow-milk cheese with a creamy, nutty taste and brown or red rind; an ideal melting or grilling cheese.

goat's made from goat's milk, has an earthy, strong taste; available in both soft and firm textures, in various shapes and sizes, and sometimes rolled in ash or herbs.

gorgonzola a creamy Italian blue cheese with a mild, sweet taste; good as an accompaniment to fruit or used to flavour sauces (especially pasta).

gruyère a hard-rind Swiss cheese with small holes and a nutty, slightly salty flavour. A popular cheese for soufflés.

haloumi a firm, cream-coloured sheep-milk cheese matured in brine; haloumi can be grilled or fried, briefly, without breaking down. Should be eaten while still warm as it becomes tough and rubbery on cooling.

mascarpone an Italian fresh cultured-cream product made in much the same way as yoghurt. Whiteish to creamy yellow in colour, with a buttery-rich, luscious texture.

mozzarella soft, spun-curd cheese; originating in southern Italy where it was traditionally made from water-buffalo milk. Now generally made from cow's milk, it is the most popular pizza cheese because of its low melting point and elasticity when heated.

parmesan also called parmigiano; is a hard, grainy cow-milk cheese originating in Italy.

ricotta a soft, sweet, moist, white cow-milk cheese with a low fat content and a slightly grainy texture. The name roughly translates as 'cooked again' and refers to ricotta's manufacture from a whey that is itself a by-product of other cheese making.

CHERVIL also known as cicily; mildly fennel-flavoured member of the parsley family with curly dark-green leaves. Available both fresh and dried.

CHICKPEAS (GARBANZO BEANS) an irregularly round, sandy-coloured legume. Has a firm texture even after cooking, a floury mouth-feel and robust nutty flavour; available canned or dried (soak for several hours in cold water before use).

CHILLI use rubber gloves when seeding and chopping fresh chillies as they can burn your skin.

cayenne pepper a thin-fleshed, long, extremely hot dried red chilli, usually purchased ground.

chipotle pronounced cheh-pote-lay. The name used for jalapeño chillies once they've been dried and smoked. Having a deep, intensely smokey flavour, rather than a searing heat, chipotles are dark brown, almost black in colour and wrinkled in appearance.

flakes also sold as crushed chilli; dehydrated deep-red extremely fine slices and whole seeds.

jalapeño pronounced hah-lah-pain-yo. Fairly hot, medium-sized, plump, dark green chilli; available pickled, sold canned or bottled, and fresh, from greengrocers.

long red available both fresh and dried; a generic term used for any moderately hot, long, thin chilli (about 6cm to 8cm long).

powder the Asian variety is the hottest, made from dried ground thai chillies; can be used instead of fresh in the proportion of ½ teaspoon chilli powder to 1 medium chopped fresh red chilli.

sauce, sweet comparatively mild, fairly sticky and runny bottled sauce made from red chillies, sugar, garlic and white vinegar; used in Thai cooking.

thai (serrano) also known as "scuds"; tiny, very hot and bright red in colour.

CHINESE COOKING WINE also called shao hsing or chinese rice wine; made from fermented rice, wheat, sugar and salt with a 13.5% alcohol content. Inexpensive and found in Asian food shops; if you can't find it, replace with mirin or sherry.

CHINESE FIVE SPICE a fragrant mixture of ground cinnamon, cloves, star anise, sichuan pepper and fennel seeds. Available from most supermarkets or Asian food shops.

CHOCOLATE

dark eating (semi-sweet) is made of a high percentage of cocoa liquor and cocoa butter, and little added sugar. Unless stated otherwise, we use dark eating chocolate in this book as it's ideal for use in desserts and cakes.

white contains no cocoa solids but derives its sweet flavour from cocoa butter. Very sensitive to heat.

CINNAMON available in pieces (called sticks or quills) and ground into powder; one of the world's most common spices.

COCOA POWDER also known as unsweetened cocoa; cocoa beans (cacao seeds) that have been fermented, roasted, shelled, ground into powder then cleared of most of the fat content.

dutch cocoa treated with an alkali to neutralize its acids. It has a reddish-brown colour, mild flavour, and is easy to dissolve in liquids.

COCONUT

cream obtained commercially from the first pressing of the coconut flesh alone, without the addition of water; the second pressing (less rich) is sold as coconut milk. Available in cans and cartons at most supermarkets.

desiccated concentrated, dried, unsweetened and finely shredded coconut flesh.

milk not the liquid inside the fruit (coconut water), but the diluted liquid from the second pressing of the white flesh of a mature coconut.

CORIANDER (CILANTRO) also known as pak chee or chinese parsley; a bright-green leafy herb with a pungent flavour. Both stems and roots of coriander are also used in cooking; wash well before using. Also available ground or as seeds; these should not be substituted for fresh as the tastes are completely different.

CORNFLOUR (CORNSTARCH) available made from corn or wheat (wheaten cornflour, gluten-free, gives a lighter texture in cakes); used as a thickening agent in cooking.

CORNICHON French for gherkin, a very small variety of cucumber. Pickled, they are a traditional accompaniment to pâté; the Swiss always serve them with fondue (or raclette).

COUSCOUS a fine, grain-like cereal product made from semolina; it swells to three or four times its original size when liquid is added.

CREAM

pouring also known as pure or fresh cream. It has no additives and contains a minimum fat content of 35%.

sour a thick, commercially-cultured sour cream with a minimum fat content of 35%.

thick (double) a dolloping cream with a minimum fat content of 45%.

thickened (heavy) a whipping cream that contains a thickener. It has a minimum fat content of 35%.

CRÈME FRAÎCHE a mature, naturally fermented cream (minimum fat content 35%) having a velvety texture and slightly tangy, nutty flavour.

CUMIN also known as zeera or comino; has a spicy, nutty flavour.

CURRY LEAVES available fresh or dried and have a mild curry flavour; use like bay leaves.

CURRY PASTES some recipes in this book call for commercially prepared pastes of varying strengths and flavours. Use whichever one you feel best suits your spice-level tolerance.

massaman rich, spicy flavour reminiscent of Middle Eastern cooking; favoured by southern Thai cooks for use in hot and sour stew-like curries and satay sauces.

red a popular curry paste; a hot blend of red chilli, garlic, shallot, lemon grass, salt, galangal, shrimp paste, kaffir lime peel, coriander, cumin and paprika. It is milder than the hotter thai green curry paste.

CURRY POWDER a blend of ground spices used for making Indian and some South-East Asian dishes. Consists of dried chilli, cumin, cinnamon, coriander, fennel, mace, fenugreek, cardamom and turmeric. Available mild or hot.

DILL also known as dill weed; used fresh or dried, in seed form or ground. Its feathery, frond-like fresh leaves are grassier and more subtle than the dried version or the seeds (which slightly resemble caraway in flavour).

DUKKAH an Egyptian specialty spice mixture made up of roasted nuts, seeds and an array of aromatic spices.

EGGPLANT also called aubergine. Ranging in size from tiny to very large and in colour from pale green to deep purple.

FENNEL a white to very pale green-white, firm, crisp, roundish vegetable about 8-12cm (3¼-4¾ inches) in diameter. The bulb has a slightly sweet, anise flavour but the leaves have a much stronger taste. Also the name of dried seeds having a licorice flavour.

FENUGREEK hard, dried seed usually sold ground as an astringent spice powder. Good with seafood and in chutneys, fenugreek helps mask unpleasant odours.

FILLO PASTRY paper-thin sheets of raw pastry; brush each sheet with oil or melted butter, stack in layers, then cut and fold as directed.

FLOUR

bread also known as gluten-enriched, strong or baker's flour. Made from a wheat that has a high gluten (protein) content and is best suited for pizza and bread making: the expansion caused by the yeast and the stretchiness imposed by kneading requires a flour that is "strong" enough to handle these stresses.

plain (all-purpose) a general all-purpose wheat flour.

self-raising plain flour sifted with baking powder in the proportion of 1 cup flour to 2 teaspoons baking powder.

wholemeal also known as wholewheat flour; milled with the wheat germ so is higher in fibre and more nutritional than plain flour.

GAI LAN also known as chinese broccoli, gai larn, kanah, gai lum and chinese kale; used more for its stems than its coarse leaves.

GARAM MASALA a blend of spices including cardamom, cinnamon, cloves, coriander, fennel and cumin, roasted and ground together. Black pepper and chilli can be added for a hotter version.

GHEE a type of clarified butter where the milk solids are cooked until they are a golden brown, which imparts a nutty flavour and sweet aroma; this fat has a high smoking point so can be heated to a high temperature without burning. Used as a cooking medium in most Indian recipes. Available from Indian supermarkets.

GINGER

fresh also called green or root ginger; the thick gnarled root of a tropical plant.

glacé fresh ginger root preserved in sugar syrup; crystallised ginger (sweetened with cane sugar) can be substituted if rinsed with warm water and dried before using.

ground also called powdered ginger; used as a flavouring in baking but cannot be substituted for fresh ginger.

GLUCOSE SYRUP also known as liquid glucose, made from wheat starch; used in jam and confectionery making. Available at health-food stores and supermarkets.

GRAVY POWDER an instant gravy mix made with browned flour. Plain flour can be used instead for thickening. Available from supermarkets in a variety of flavours.

HONEY the variety sold in a squeezable container is not suitable for the recipes in this book.

KAFFIR LIME LEAVES also known as bai magrood. Aromatic leaves of a citrus tree; two glossy dark green leaves joined end to end, forming a rounded hourglass shape. A strip of fresh lime peel may be substituted for each kaffir lime leaf.

KUMARA (ORANGE SWEET POTATO) the Māori name of an orange-fleshed sweet potato often confused with yam.

LEMON GRASS a tall, clumping, lemon-smelling and -tasting, sharp-edged grass; the white part of the stem is used, finely chopped, in cooking.

LENTILS (red, brown, yellow) dried pulses often identified by and named after their colour; also known as dhal.

french-style green are a local cousin to the famous (and expensive) French lentils du puy; green-blue, tiny lentils with a nutty, earthy flavour and a hardy nature that allows them to be rapidly cooked without disintegrating.

MAPLE SYRUP, PURE distilled from the sap of sugar maple trees found only in Canada and the USA. Maple-flavoured syrup or pancake syrup is not an adequate substitute for the real thing.

MARSALA a fortified Italian wine produced in the region surrounding the Sicilian city of Marsala; recognisable by its intense amber colour and complex aroma. Often used in cooking.

MILK we use full-cream homogenised milk unless otherwise specified.

buttermilk in spite of its name, buttermilk is actually low in fat, varying between 0.6% and 2.0% per 100ml. Originally the term given to the slightly sour liquid left after butter was churned from cream, today it is intentionally made from no-fat or low-fat milk to which specific bacterial cultures have been added during the manufacturing process.

sweetened condensed a canned milk product consisting of milk with more than half the water content removed and sugar added to the remaining milk.

MIXED SPICE a classic spice mixture generally containing caraway, allspice, coriander, cumin, nutmeg and ginger, although cinnamon and other spices can be added. It is used with fruit and in cakes.

MUSHROOMS

button small, cultivated white mushrooms with a mild flavour. When a recipe in this book calls for an unspecified type of mushroom, use button.

flat large, flat mushrooms with a rich earthy flavour. They are sometimes misnamed field mushrooms, which are wild mushrooms.

shiitake also known as chinese black, forest or golden oak mushrooms; although cultivated, they are large and meaty and have the earthiness and taste of wild mushrooms.

swiss brown also known as cremini or roman mushrooms; are light brown mushrooms with a full-bodied flavour.

MUSTARD

dijon also called french. Pale brown, creamy, distinctively flavoured, fairly mild French mustard.

wholegrain also known as seeded. A French-style coarse-grain mustard made from crushed mustard seeds and dijon-style french mustard. Works well with cold meats and sausages

NOODLES

fresh rice also called ho fun, khao pun, sen yau, pho or kway tiau, depending on the country of manufacture. Can be purchased in strands of various widths or large sheets weighing about 500g which are to be cut into the desired noodle size. Chewy and pure white, they do not need pre-cooking before use.

rice stick also known assen lek, ho fun or kway teow; especially popular South-East Asian dried rice noodles. They come in different widths (thin used in soups, wide in stir-fries), but all should be soaked in hot water to soften.

rice vermicelli also known as sen mee, mei fun or bee hoon. Used throughout Asia in spring rolls and cold salads; similar to bean threads, only longer and made with rice flour instead of mung bean starch. Before using, soak the dried noodles in hot water until softened, boil them briefly then rinse with hot water.

OIL

olive made from ripened olives. Extra virgin and virgin are the first and second press, respectively, of the olives; "light" refers to taste not fat levels.

peanut pressed from ground peanuts; most commonly used oil in Asian cooking because of its high smoke point (capacity to handle high heat without burning).

sesame used as a flavouring rather than a cooking medium.

vegetable oils sourced from plant rather than animal fats.

ONIONS

baby also called pickling and cocktail onions; are baby brown onions but are larger than shallots. To peel, cover with boiling water and stand for 2 minutes, then drain. The skins will slip off easily.

brown and white interchangeable; white onions have a more pungent flesh.

green (scallions) also called, incorrectly, shallot; an immature onion picked before the bulb has formed, has a long, bright-green edible stalk.

red also known as spanish, red spanish or bermuda onion; a sweet-flavoured, large, purple-red onion.

shallots also called french or golden shallots or eschalots; small and elongated with a brown skin.

spring an onion with a small white bulb and long, narrow green-leafed tops.

PASSATA sieved tomato puree. To substitute, puree and sieve canned tomatoes or use canned tomato puree which is similar, but slightly thicker.

PINE NUTS not a nut but a small, cream-coloured kernel from pine cones. Toast before use to bring out their flavour.

POLENTA also known as cornmeal; a flour-like cereal made of ground corn (maize). Also the name of the dish made from it.

QUINCE yellow-skinned fruit with hard texture and astringent, tart taste; eaten cooked or as a preserve. Long, slow cooking makes the flesh a deep rose pink.

SOY SAUCE made from fermented soya beans. Several variations are available in most supermarkets and Asian food stores. We use japanese soy sauce unless stated otherwise.

SUGAR

brown very soft, finely granulated sugar retaining molasses for its characteristic colour and flavour.

caster (superfine) finely granulated table sugar.

demerara small-grained golden-coloured crystal sugar.

icing (confectioners') also known as powdered sugar; pulverised granulated sugar crushed together with a small amount of cornflour (cornstarch).

palm also called nam tan pip, jaggery, jawa or gula melaka; made from the sap of the sugar palm tree. Light brown to black in colour and usually sold in rock-hard cakes; use with brown sugar if unavailable.

white (granulated) coarse, granulated table sugar, also known as crystal sugar.

TAMARIND CONCENTRATE (or paste) the commercial result of the distillation of tamarind juice into a condensed, compacted paste.

VINEGAR

balsamic originally from Modena, Italy, there are now many balsamic vinegars on the market ranging in pungency and quality depending on how, and for how long, they have been aged. Quality can be determined up to a point by price; use the most expensive sparingly.

cider made from fermented apples.

white made from distilled grain alcohol.

WATERCRESS one of the cress family, a large group of peppery greens.

YEAST (dried and fresh) A raising agent used in dough making. Granular (7g sachets) and fresh compressed (20g blocks) yeast can almost always be substituted for the other when yeast is called for.

YOGHURT, GREEK-STYLE plain yoghurt strained in a cloth (muslin) to remove the whey and to give it a creamy consistency.

ZUCCHINI also called courgette; small, pale- or dark-green or yellow vegetable of the squash family. Harvested when young, its edible flowers can be stuffed and deep-fried.

Conversion chart

MEASURES

One Australian metric measuring cup holds approximately 250ml; one Australian metric tablespoon holds 20ml; one Australian metric teaspoon holds 5ml.

The difference between one country's measuring cups and another's is within a two- or three-teaspoon variance, and will not affect your cooking results. North America, New Zealand and the United Kingdom use a 15ml tablespoon.

All cup and spoon measurements are level. The most accurate way of measuring dry ingredients is to weigh them. When measuring liquids, use a clear glass or plastic jug with the metric markings.

The imperial measurements used in these recipes are approximate only. Measurements for cake pans are approximate only. Using same-shaped cake pans of a similar size should not affect the outcome of your baking. We measure the inside top of the cake pan to determine sizes.

We use large eggs with an average weight of 60g.

DRY MEASURES

METRIC	IMPERIAL
15G	½OZ
30G	1OZ
60G	2OZ
90G	3OZ
125G	4OZ (¼LB)
155G	5OZ
185G	6OZ
220G	7OZ
250G	8OZ (½LB)
280G	9OZ
315G	10OZ
345G	11OZ
375G	12OZ (¾LB)
410G	13OZ
440G	14OZ
470G	15OZ
500G	16OZ (1LB)
750G	24OZ (1½LB)
1KG	32OZ (2LB)

LIQUID MEASURES

METRIC	IMPERIAL
30ML	1 FLUID OZ
60ML	2 FLUID OZ
100ML	3 FLUID OZ
125ML	4 FLUID OZ
150ML	5 FLUID OZ
190ML	6 FLUID OZ
250ML	8 FLUID OZ
300ML	10 FLUID OZ
500ML	16 FLUID OZ
600ML	20 FLUID OZ
1000ML (1 LITRE)	1¾ PINTS

LENGTH MEASURES

METRIC	IMPERIAL
3MM	⅛IN
6MM	¼IN
1CM	½IN
2CM	¾IN
2.5CM	1IN
5CM	2IN
6CM	2½IN
8CM	3IN
10CM	4IN
13CM	5IN
15CM	6IN
18CM	7IN
20CM	8IN
22CM	9IN
25CM	10IN
28CM	11IN
30CM	12IN (1FT)

OVEN TEMPERATURES

The oven temperatures in this book are for conventional ovens; if you have a fan-forced oven, decrease the temperature by 10-20 degrees.

	°C (CELSIUS)	°F (FAHRENHEIT)
VERY SLOW	120	250
SLOW	150	300
MODERATELY SLOW	160	325
MODERATE	180	350
MODERATELY HOT	200	400
HOT	220	425
VERY HOT	240	475

Index

PUBLISHED IN 2016 BY BAUER MEDIA BOOKS, AUSTRALIA.
BAUER MEDIA BOOKS IS A DIVISION OF BAUER MEDIA PTY LTD.

BAUER MEDIA BOOKS

PUBLISHER
JO RUNCIMAN

EDITORIAL & FOOD DIRECTOR
PAMELA CLARK

DIRECTOR OF SALES, MARKETING & RIGHTS
BRIAN CEARNES

CREATIVE DIRECTOR & DESIGNER
HANNAH BLACKMORE

SENIOR EDITOR
STEPHANIE KISTNER

JUNIOR EDITOR
AMANDA LEES

OPERATIONS MANAGER
DAVID SCOTTO

FOOD EDITORS
LOUISE PATNIOTIS, REBECCA MELI

RECIPE DEVELOPERS
CHARLOTTE BINNS-MCDONALD,
SARAH MURPHY, NADIA FONOFF,
KIRSTEN JENKINS, KATHY KNUDSEN

PHOTOGRAPHER
JAMES MOFFATT

STYLIST
OLIVIA BLACKMORE

PHOTOCHEF
ANGELA DEVLIN

WITH THANKS TO OUR MODELS
SHELLY SHINE, SIMON SHINE,
ABBY SMART, CLARE GIBSON

WITH THANKS TO OUR LOCATION
JUSTINE RAMSAY; LOUGHMORE COTTAGES,
164 MOSS VALE RD, KANGAROO VALLEY,
NSW 2577
WWW.LOUGHMORECOTTAGES.COM

PRINTED IN CHINA
BY LEO PAPER PRODUCTS LTD

TITLE: FOOD FOR THE SOUL / PAMELA CLARK.
ISBN: 9781742457093 (HARDBACK)
SUBJECTS: COMFORT FOOD.
COOKING.
OTHER CREATORS/CONTRIBUTORS:
CLARK, PAMELA, EDITOR.
ALSO TITLED: AUSTRALIAN WOMEN'S WEEKLY.
DEWEY NUMBER: 641.5

© BAUER MEDIA PTY LIMITED 2016
ABN 18 053 273 546

PUBLISHED BY BAUER MEDIA BOOKS,
A DIVISION OF BAUER MEDIA PTY LTD,
54 PARK ST, SYDNEY; GPO BOX 4088,
SYDNEY, NSW 2001, AUSTRALIA
PH +61 2 9282 8618; FAX +61 2 9126 3702
WWW.AWWCOOKBOOKS.COM.AU

ORDER BOOKS
PHONE 136 116 (WITHIN AUSTRALIA)

OR ORDER ONLINE AT
WWW.AWWCOOKBOOKS.COM.AU

SEND RECIPE ENQUIRIES TO
RECIPEENQUIRIES@BAUER-MEDIA.COM.AU